T0236395

Communications in Computer and Information Science   514

Commenced Publication in 2007
Founding and Former Series Editors:
Alfredo Cuzzocrea, Dominik Ślęzak, and Xiaokang Yang

More information about this series at http://www.springer.com/series/7899

Ross Horne (Ed.)

Embracing Global Computing in Emerging Economies

First Workshop, EGC 2015
Almaty, Kazakhstan, February 26–28, 2015
Proceedings

 Springer

Editor
Ross Horne
Kazakh-British Technical University
Almaty
Kazakhstan

ISSN 1865-0929   ISSN 1865-0937   (electronic)
Communications in Computer and Information Science
ISBN 978-3-319-25042-7   ISBN 978-3-319-25043-4   (eBook)
DOI 10.1007/978-3-319-25043-4

Library of Congress Control Number: 2015952998

Springer Cham Heidelberg New York Dordrecht London

Printed on acid-free paper

Springer International Publishing AG Switzerland is part of Springer Science+Business Media
(www.springer.com)

Preface

This volume contains papers presented at ECG 2015: Embracing Global Computing in Emerging Economies held during February 26–28, 2015, in Almaty, Kazakhstan.

There were 25 submissions. Each submission went through two phases of reviewing: the first phase being before the workshop; and the second phase beginning one month after the workshop. Each paper was reviewed by on average 2.3 Programme Committee members, with accepted papers receiving three reviews. The committee decided to accept 14 papers for presentation at the workshop and 10 papers for these proceedings. Three papers by invited speakers also appear: in particular, papers by networking and distributed computing experts Yehia Elkhatib and Gareth Tyson from Lancaster University and Queen Mary. respectively; and by theoretician Nikolay Shilov from A. P. Ershov Institute of Informatics in Novosibirsk.

The computer science workshop "Embracing Global Computing in Emerging Economies" was co-located with the economics workshop "The Impact of Emerging Economies and Their Multinational Enterprises on the World Economy" supported by a Researcher Links workshop grant from the British Council. The workshop was also partially funded by the Faculty of Information Technology and Business School at Kazakh-British Technical University. Registration was free to participants, and grants covering travel and expenses were awarded to participants with accepted or invited papers.

The workshop focused on modern problems in computing particular to relevant emerging economies such as Kazakhstan. Kazakhstan is a region with high investment and a well-educated workforce. However, the remote location of Kazakhstan compared with the world's datacenters raises challenges for organisations making the transition to cloud computing. Cloud computing brings serious economic and technological benefits, including the immediate scalability of resources on demand and the high availability through a global network of data centres. Issues such as low population density, poor communications infrastructure, and vulnerability to natural disasters augment the risk of investing in Kazakhstan's IT industry and supported services. The workshop aims to boost innovation by identifying relevant research problems, providing a forum for cross-sector interaction, and a platform where experienced and early-stage researchers can comfortably interact.

The papers contained in this volume are relevant to the themes of the workshop in two ways: they are directly relevant to the problems of delivering cloud services in an emerging economy such as Kazakhstan; or they represent ICT innovation by scientists in the region. The directly relevant papers are those by Elkhatib, Tyson et al., Shilov, Abdrau, Popa et al., Trubitsin, Hadley et al., and Aman et al.. The papers indirectly relevant require a little more justification. The paper by Sarbasova et al. proposes an approach that can be applied to medical diagnosis over a cloud and mobile-based infrastructure, thereby reaching remote underprivileged regions. The paper by Umarov et al. presents a data-centric methodology developed by scientists in Kazakhstan. The paper by Kornev is applicable to industry. The paper by Fish et al. represents a cluster of theoreticians operational in Kazakhstan. Finally, the paper by Bakibayev et al. presents ICT support for a real problem faced by city planners; indeed a related bus route opened in Almaty in the time between the workshop and the production of these proceedings.

The workshop featured speakers and panelists from industry including Sergey Khalyapin representing Citrix, Moscow; Olzhas Tolegen representing Microsoft, Kazakhstan; and Dias Kadyrov representing EMC, Kazakhstan. The third and final day of the workshop focused on an invited talk from Sergey Khalyapin followed by a panel discussion featuring invited academics and professionals from industry. The panel discussion addressed the challenges involved in building data centres in Kazakhstan. The three companies represented are currently making strategic investments in cloud infrastructure and expertise in Kazakhstan, while several of the academics have been investigating community-driven alternatives to data centers. The problem that emerged was a need to quantify the risk of investing in data centers in Kazakhstan, taking into account the geographic and economic context. Stimulating dialog between industry and academia is an important step towards increased innovation.

We would like, firstly, to thank our Programme Committee, who have worked to tight deadlines to evaluate and provide constructive feedback to authors. We would also like to mention the members of the Faculty of Information Technology and Business School who contributed actively in the run-up to the workshop. We are particularly grateful to our good friend Prof. Ken Chairman, who suggested that the Faculty of Information Technology and Business School should combine efforts to maximise the impact of this event. We would like to acknowledge financial support from the British Council, who covered travel and expenses, and Kazakh-British Technical University, who financed refreshments and facilities for the event. We would like to mention the invaluable mentoring in preparation for this event received by esteemed members of the international scientific community, particularly Prof. Vladimiro Sassone, Prof. Alexander Romanovsky, and Prof. Gordon Blair. Last but not least, we would like to mention our team of graduate student helpers, who demonstrated a keen understanding of the necessity for further research while enabling the organisers to enjoy the workshop.

May 2015   Ross Horne

Organisation

Programme Committee

Assel Akzhalova	Kazakh-British Technical University, Kazakhstan
Bogdan Aman	Romanian Academy, Iasi, Romania
Gabrielle Anderson	University College London, UK
Lyazzat Atymtayeva	Kazakh-British Technical University, Kazakhstan
Timur Bakibayev	ADA University, Baku, Azerbaijan
Kenes Beketayev	Lawrence Berkeley National Laboratory, USA
Gabriel Ciobanu	Romanian Academy, Iasi, Romania
Yehia Elkhatib	Lancaster University, UK
Ross Horne	Kazakh-British Technical University, Kazakhstan
Ramesh Kini	Kazakh-British Technical University, Kazakhstan
Shekoufeh Kolandouzrahimi	Kings College London, UK
Anatoly Kornev	Kazakh-British Technical University, Kazakhstan
Sofoklis Makridis	University of Bolton, UK
Denis Nicole	University of Southampton, UK
Alexander Romanovsky	Newcastle University, UK
Asieh Salehi Fathabadi	University of Southampton, UK
Vladimiro Sassone	University of Southampton, UK
Nikolay Shilov	Nazarbayev University, Kazakhstan
Asqar Shotqara	Kazakh-British Technical University, Kazakhstan
Timur Umarov	Kazakh-British Technical University, Kazakhstan
Toby Wilkinson	University of Southampton, UK
Damir Yeliussizov	Kazakh-British Technical University, Kazakhstan

Contents

Building Cloud Applications for Challenged Networks

Yehia Elkhatib[✉]

School of Computing and Communications, Lancaster University, Lancaster, UK
y.elkhatib@lancaster.ac.uk

Abstract. Cloud computing has seen vast advancements and uptake in many parts of the world. However, many of the design patterns and deployment models are not very suitable for locations with challenged networks such as countries with no nearby datacenters. This paper describes the problem and discusses the options available for such locations, focusing specifically on community clouds as a short-term solution. The paper highlights the impact of recent trends in the development of cloud applications and how changing these could better help deployment in challenged networks. The paper also outlines the consequent challenges in bridging different cloud deployments, also known as *cross-cloud computing*.

1 Introduction

Cloud computing is yet another step on the quest for holy grail of computing as described by John MacCarthy whilst addressing the MIT Centennial in 1961:

> *If computers of the kind I have advocated become the computers of the future, then computing may someday be organized as a public utility just as the telephone system is a public utility... The computer utility could become the basis of a new and important industry.*

Indeed, the cloud computing market is a vast and rapidly expanding one, worth $58bn in 2013 and expected to grow to $191bn by 2020 [19]. It offers its users unparalleled flexibility and scalability, allowing them to easily and feasibly scale a system up and down to meet changing business targets (e.g. customer demand), to dynamically mitigate system failures through the spawning of new servers, and to expeditiously and seamlessly roll out new capabilities. This allows businesses to curb computing expenses whilst still supporting agile business progress. For researchers, it imposes much lower resource provisioning barriers that the closest alternatives (HPC or grid): virtually immediate resource provisioning, huge scale to store and process vast observational datasets, and less restrictions on location. This enables researchers using the cloud to focus on their processes rather than on the computing infrastructure, and to run computations and access data when and where they require.

© Springer International Publishing Switzerland 2015
R. Horne (Ed.): EGC 2015, CCIS 514, pp. 1–10, 2015.
DOI: 10.1007/978-3-319-25043-4_1

2   Problem Space

First, one needs to define the term *emerging economies* in order to add some
clarity, albeit in the boundaries of this work, to such usually loosely defined
term. An emerging economy (EE) is one with a relatively stable government,
growing investment in public infrastructure, and a prospering consumer market
typically manifested by an expanding middle class with increasing levels of dis-
posable income. Under such definition, example os EEs include countries like
Kazakhstan, Malaysia and Turkey.

In EEs, access to resources is not the main obstacle in the way to encour-
age uptake of the cloud. On the contrary, both infrastructure provisions and
end user devices are fairly affordable for a large fraction of the local population. The main problem is to do with the network connection. This is a problem
because currently all applications are distributed [7]. This is partly due to an
ever increasing reliance on communication between applications to carry out
transactions, and on interaction between users for social and productivity purposes. This is also due to a shift in application provisioning: most applications
are now hosted remotely and delivered remotely to the end users. Gone are the
days of shrink-wrapped software.

Such shift introduces an increasing expectation on good network performance, which many locations do not have. In this paper, I focus on such locations
with challenged network connections.

3   Latency Is High, So What?

Making more bandwidth is easy [8], which is why Internet Service Providers
(ISPs) all around the world will always market their services based on bandwidth.
However, having more bandwidth does not always translate to better network
performance [4]. On the other hand, decreasing network latency is much more
effective in increasing application throughput [12]. In this regard, significant
efforts in the network research community specifically target the issue of inflated
network latency. A recent example of this is SPDY [2], a web protocol that
multiplexes HTTP connections to reduce the number of round trips between
client and server. This, however, is only effective in reducing the bursty nature
of HTTP for certain network connections [10].

High network latency has an obvious detrimental effect on latency-sensitive
applications. In the gaming industry, 100 ms is considered to be the threshold between an interactive and unresponsive experience [9,17]. For Voice over IP
(VoIP), the threshold is between 100 ms [27] and 150 ms [15] for acceptable audio
transmission. On e-commerce websites, increments of just 100 ms can decrease
sales by 1 % [18]. Similarly, it is reported that most web users would not tolerate beyond 2 s "for simple information retrieval tasks on the Web" [22], which
demands significantly low latency between the client and the different servers
serving different pieces of content on a typical webpage.

Even bandwidth-hungry applications, such as video streaming, can be
adversely affected by relatively high delay levels. Tuning TCP send and receive

buffers ensures that the amount of data in transit at any time is the maximum that the link between the sender and receiver could accommodate. Untuned TCP buffers fails to attain the maximum achievable throughput. Despite the knowledge of this fact in the networking community for many years (cf. [20]), manually optimising TCP buffers requires good technical nous [11]. Various efforts over the years attempt to move away from the black art of manual TCP tuning to automatically adjusted TCP buffer sizes and other networking parameters based on connection characteristics [28,33,34]. Nonetheless, such solutions are still not included by default in modern operating systems.

4   Design Principles

In this section, I revisit some of the fundamental design principles of modern day distributed systems in light of the constraints imposed by challenged networks. I propose alternative design choices for each principle, giving examples where possible.

4.1   Application Signalling

One of the unintentional products of the easy integration facilitated by cloud computing services is a move towards building *chatty applications*. These are applications that interact with each other at a high network cost manifested as a very high number of messages and/or large message sizes.

Such verbosity is partly due to a high skewness in the cloud application space. I conjecture that this a by-product of the startup culture, where most applications are built in order to be sold to a much larger company or get funds from a venture capitalist. Under such conditions services are engineered to demonstrate high impact and revenue. Hence, the majority of applications emanating from the silicon valleys of the world are developed for the highly connected metropolises in the industrialised world where they originate; e.g. San Francisco, New York, London, etc.

Hidden within this context is an obvious assumption of relative proximity to industrial-scale data centers. At the same time, cloud service providers (CSPs) over provision their services to be able to handle a thick and fast stream of incoming API calls. Hence, the only cost for verbose API interactions is monetary. The cost models of major CSPs make this relatively affordable for most applications anyway. This is the root of the recent emergence of chatty applications. Loose-coupling is only really considered when it starts to be too expensive to shift large data sets or when it becomes difficult (or impossible) to handle large volumes of updates.

However, this is not suitable for EEs with relatively high RTT where network communication has to be rationed. Therefore, it is important to design applications that can cope with high latency, i.e. have low signalling or "less chatty" as a design requirement. In this light, the communication style of the application is expected to lean more towards asynchronicity. For example, 'fire and forget' asynchronous remote procedure calls (RPC) is much more suitable than the currently common trend of blocking whilst an API call is completed. Similarly, message oriented middleware (MOM) solutions offer loosely-coupled communications with little time guarantees.

4.2 Data Exchange

One result of the assumption of proximity to data centres is diminishing the third tier in the classical 3-tier distributed systems model: the data tier. Instead, a lot of the data is constantly being sent over the network back and forth between machines and clients as and when required. The data tier, typically a relational or a NoSQL database, is only used for huge bulks of data. This trend if facilitated by the Representational State Transfer (REST) architectural design principles [13]. Indeed, it suits the cloud as we now know it: Web services are completely stateless and hence have less load on them. Clients invoke services with the data required to transition between different states. Virtual machines (VMs) hosting the web services are easily replaceable and replicatable. This vastly improves scalability and simplifies infrastructure management tasks such as load balancing and failure recovery.

For EEs, the data tier needs to be reinstated at least for deployments in challenged network conditions. This is manifested as separate replicas that are more geared towards the users it serves, perhaps based on geographical location. Restricting write updates based on domain is an obvious policy to minimise write-write conflicts between different replicas. Lazy updates with remote replicas would be sufficient for most applications, however this is discussed in more detail in the following subsection. Such setup still preserves the ability to create large application platforms that are made up of stateless VMs that are easy to spin up or stop as and when required, whilst also maintaining a certain degree of independence on data exchange over WAN links of relatively low performance levels.

4.3 Data Repositories

The famous Brewer's (or CAP) theorem states that a database system can attain a maximum of two of the following three objectives: consistency, availability, and partition tolerance [5]. In traditional distributed database systems, consistency and partition tolerance were valued more than availability. In contrast, the stateless nature of many cloud applications forsakes consistency, and instead prioritises availability and partition tolerance. We see this reflected in the popularity of many 'eventually consistent' NoSQL systems such as Cassandra, Couchbase, Dynamo, MongoDB, Riak, and more.

For applications in network challenged areas, partition tolerance has to be the highest priority. This is to allow the system to continue operation if network connectivity is lost or is of poor quality. The trade-off, then, becomes between availability and consistency. This is dependent on the application in hand. For some applications, such as social networks and multimedia systems, availability is perhaps more important than consistency with the rest of the remote system. On the other hand, applications such as e-commerce and customer relationship management would place consistency as a higher priority as asynchronous transaction could cost more than a missed one. As such, data repositories need to be engineered in such a way to cater for both the needs of the application and the restrictions imposed by the deployment environment.

4.4 Communication Protocols

The TCP/IP stack has become an entrenched part of most distributed systems we have today. On top of this, HTTP and HTTPS have also become a de facto communication standards for the majority of cloud applications and APIs [25]. However, this protocol stack needs to be reconsidered to confirm suitability for the target deployment environment, alongside TCP optimisations discussed in Sect. 3. Note that networking stack used to interconnect system elements could be different from that enabling user access.

For instance, SPDY (and more recently HTTP/2.0) offer better performance by multiplexing different data streams between two hosts (such as a client and a server) onto one TCP connection. This saves significant amount of unnecessary connection establishment time, which brings considerable improvements especially over network links with high latency [10]. However, it is also susceptible to performance degradation on links with relatively high loss rate [ibid].

The IP protocol is the default choice for traditional host address-oriented network architectures. However, alternative network addressing paradigms could offer alternative solutions that might be more suitable for challenged networks. An example of this is information-centric networking (ICN) [16,31]. To date, only one large-scale simulation study is available as evidence of ICN's promise [30] but is focused on caching content in a peer-to-peer information exchange network. Studies tailored specifically for the conditions of challenged networks would be very useful.

5 Discussion

In this section, I discuss two main approaches to solving the challenges highlighted in the paper thus far.

5.1 Top-Down Approach

An answer to the challenges to distributed systems in EEs as highlighted above is to build local or regional data centers. This is indeed a comprehensive solution that is worth investigating, especially with the special context of many EEs that dictates possible innovations such as using alternative energy sources. However, such solution involves huge long-term projects that require large budgets, significant depth and range of expertise, and long-term geopolitical planning. In other words, it will not bring instant solutions to people needing to access cloud resources in the short term.

5.2   Bottom-Up Approach

An alternative strategy is to provide relatively low-cost systems that are rapidly realisable, even if they only offer partial solutions. The concept of community clouds offers a rewarding option in this regard.

Community clouds is a cooperative model for deploying clouds driven by certain restrictions. In the context discussed here, the constraint is limited connectivity. The model relies on using free open source software solutions and affordable hardware to provide a self-service infrastructure. It is similar in spirit to the cooperative models of wireless mesh networks and volunteer computing (e.g. SETI@Home, BOINC). A typical setup would use OpenStack over a small set of commodity hardware machines. This brings relatively rapid access to cloud resources as well as active involvement in assembly and operation.

Examples of innovative community cloud solutions are starting to emerge. Of these, I present only three for illustration purposes.

Cloud&Heat Technologies[1] [1] is a German company offering mini-clouds that recycle the heat they emitted. A mini-cloud is a set of self-contained fire-proof cabinets that are installed in the basements of residential and commercial buildings. They comprise of between one and six cabinets that operate as a single OpenStack deployment connected by broadband to the wider Internet. The deployment is capable of operating a range of cloud appliances obtained via the Bitnami open source marketplace. The heat produced by the cabinets is used to warm a water buffer tank for domestic purposes (e.g. washing) and central heating radiators.

Another example linked to energy efficiency in domestic environments comes from Qarnot[2]. This French company designed a domestic central heating radiator module that is in fact a multi-processor HPC cluster. The objective is to attract intensive computing jobs to locations where heat is needed. When the user turns up the thermostat, enough extra computation is directed from corporate clients to increase the emitted heat at the user's location. Additional electricity costs required for carrying out the computation are refunded to the user. The Qarnot cluster supports different job types of scientific applications, such as AutoDock, Blender, Gromacs, NAMD, NWChem, OpenFOAM, Python, Quantum Espresso, and R.

A third example targets ad hoc cloud deployments in order to make them reliable enough for executing demanding applications. SCADAMAR [6] uses different network overlays to run MapReduce jobs over volunteer clouds. The Berkeley Open Infrastructure for Network Computing (BOINC) [3] is used to access underused resources on different devices in the volunteer cloud. BitTorrent is used as a substrate to distribute input, intermediate and output data between the nodes in the system (mappers and reducers). A bespoke scheduler is used to tolerate node failures, enabling the system to be resilient and to achieve job throughput over a potentially high number of nodes.

---

[1] http://www.cloudandheat.com/.

[2] http://www.qarnot-computing.com/.

6   Cross-Cloud Computing

The subsequent challenge is to piece the different cloud blocks together to form a larger pool of resources without barriers and with minimum gravity to any of the blocks in particular. In other words, solutions must be developed in order to enable applications to easily straddle different cloud infrastructures in a hybrid fashion, and to ease difficulties of moving between different imputing infrastructures. I refer to this challenge as 'cross-cloud computing'.

The difficulty of cross-cloud computing arises from a number of sources. There is the classical interoperability problem, manifested here in the form of APIs that are divergent both semantically and syntactically. There is also a significant obstacle in porting applications between cloud infrastructures due to the different formats used to capture the state of running and idle VMs, as well as due to the high network overhead associated with such migration practices. In the following, I give an overview of the migration options as they currently stand and the possible improvements that could be delivered to alleviate some of the problems in this area.

6.1   Entry

Developers wishing to enter the cloud market are faced with an array of questions that are in some cases quite difficult to answer: *(a)*Which provider? *(b)* Which instance type(s)? *(c)* Which availability zone? *(d)* What time? This is complicated with an overwhelmingly large range of options for each question. Moreover, the answers to these questions are quite subjective but would greatly determine the incurred cost and performance of the application. Hence, work is required to aid developers decide the best deployment environment for their application and to re-evaluate such decisions as the application requirements and the cloud market offerings change. Some work is already starting to happen in this area, e.g. [23, 26, 32].

The concern of divergent APIs could be sufficiently addressed for many use cases by employing any of the number of multi-cloud common programming models or libraries available for such purpose. These include jclouds[3], Brooklyn[4], Scalr[5], SeaClouds [24], and others. They provide a 'least common denominator' between the different APIs which, as already mentioned, is sufficient for many cloud application developers whose intent does not exceed starting and stopping instances. However, any need outside the least common denominator API, e.g. billing, is not supported and needs to be addressed individually by the developer. This obviously detracts from the value of such solutions.

---

[3] http://jclouds.apache.org/.
[4] https://brooklyn.incubator.apache.org/.
[5] http://www.scalr.com/.

6.2   Migration

To port a workload between different cloud infrastructures, the options are currently as follows. One could package memory and disk state along with associated metadata onto a virtual disk image and transfer that across. This is the most network expensive method as such 'pre-baked VM images' could be a few gigabytes in size. In addition, different cloud providers accept different sets of machine image formats.

An alternative is to use configuration management tools (CMTs), such as Chef[6] and Ansible[7]. These allow a developer to express in code what their application needs in terms of number of instances and the software that needs to be set on each instance. Despite quite promising in theory, they are not as deterministic as one would want them to be as there are non-reconcilable differences in the results achieved over varying operating systems [35]. Another hidden cost is developer time: CMTs offer no error diagnosis or remediation support if the desired execution environment is not produced. Instead, the developer has to revert to manual modifications.

A third approach is to replace reliance on VMs by employing containers as lightweight isolated execution environments. Despite being established in the Linux community for years (cf. [29]), containers as a concept have gained significant attention in recent months due to the rise of technologies such as Docker [21] and Rocket[8]. These provide developers with very accessible and controlled means of packaging and distributing software over lightweight OS-supported containers. This is indeed very useful for testing and rolling out new services. However, they are designed for immutable appliances and as such are not suitable for migrating stateful appliances that are in operation. An alternative is MultiBox [14] which utilises only Linux-native features to support minimalist containers to decouple guest processes from the host machine. This offers a migration vehicle that is completely independent of the CSP as long as they provide Linux VMs on top of which MultiBox could operate.

7   Conclusion

Cloud computing offers great potential for building elastic and agile applications in different sectors. There are additional challenges to capitalising on this potential for those wanting to deploy cloud applications under challenged network conditions. In this paper, I focused specifically on the case of emerging economies. I highlighted network latency as the main problem with such environments, and I discussed how the design and implementation of cloud applications need to be consequently changed. I then presented an overview of community clouds as a feasible short-term solution for founding cloud infrastructures in a grassroots fashion. Finally, I identified cross-cloud computing as the key future challenge in

---

[6] https://www.chef.io/.

[7] http://www.ansible.com/.

[8] https://coreos.com/blog/rocket/.

terms of breaking down the barriers between such grassroots deployments, and also to open then up to the rest of the global cloud ecosystem.

Acknowledgments. The author is grateful for the organisers of the International Workshop on Embracing Global Computing in Emerging Economies, and in particular Dr. Ross Horne, for their invitation to present and discuss an earlier version of this work. This work was supported in part by the CHIST-ERA Dionasys project grant reference EP/M015734/1.

References

1. Cloud&Heat - the efficient cloud service. http://www.cloudandheat.com/
2. SPDY: An experimental protocol for a faster web. http://www.chromium.org/spdy/spdy-whitepaper
3. Anderson, D.P.: BOINC: a system for public-resource computing and storage. In: Fifth IEEE/ACM International Workshop on Grid Computing, pp. 4–10, November 2004
4. Belshe, M.: More bandwidth doesn't matter (much). Google Inc. (2010)
5. Brewer, E.: CAP twelve years later: how the "rules" have changed. Computer **45**(2), 23–29 (2012)
6. Bruno, R., Ferreira, P.: SCADAMAR: Scalable and data-efficient internet mapreduce. In: Proceedings of the CrossCloud Brokers International Workshop, pp. 2:1–2:6. ACM, December 2014
7. Cavage, M.: There's just no getting around it: You're building a distributed system. Queue **11**(4), 30–41 (2013)
8. Cheshire, S.: It's the latency, stupid, May 1996. http://www.stuartcheshire.org/rants/Latency.html
9. Claypool, M., Claypool, K.: Latency and player actions in online games. Commun. ACM **49**(11), 40–45 (2006)
10. Elkhatib, Y., Tyson, G., Welzl, M.: Can SPDY really make the web faster?. In: Proceedings of IFIP International Conference on Networking, June 2014
11. Mahdavi, J., et al.: Enabling high performance data transfers. http://www.psc.edu/index.php/networking/641-tcp-tune
12. Fall, K., McCanne, S.: You don't know jack about network performance. Queue **3**(4), 54–59 (2005)
13. Fielding, R.T.: Architectural Styles and the Design of Network-based Software Architectures. Ph.D. thesis. University of California, Irvine (2000)
14. Hadley, J., Elkhatib, Y., Blair, G.S., Roedig, U.: Multibox: lightweight containers for vendor-independent multi-cloud deployments. In: Horne, R. (ed.): EGC 2015, CCIS 514, pp. 1–12 (2015)
15. International Telecommunication Union. Recommendation G.114: One-way transmission time, May 2003
16. Jacobson, V., Smetters, D.K., Thornton, J.D., Plass, M.F., Briggs, N.H., Braynard, R.L.: Networking named content. In: Proceedings of the 5th International Conference on Emerging Networking Experiments and Technologies, CoNEXT 2009, pp. 1–12. ACM (2009)
17. Jarschel, M., Schlosser, D., Scheuring, S., Hossfeld, T.: An evaluation of QoE in cloud gaming based on subjective tests. In: International Conference on Innovative Mobile and Internet Services in Ubiquitous Computing (IMIS), pp. 330–335, June 2011

18. Kohavi, R., Longbotham, R.: Online experiments: lessons learned. Computer **40**(9), 103–105 (2007)
19. KPMG. Cloud survey report: Elevating business in the cloud, October 2014. http://www.kpmginfo.com/EnablingBusinessInTheCloud/downloads/2014%20KPMG%20Cloud%20Survey%20Report%20-%20Final%2012-10-14.pdf
20. Lakshman, T., Madhow, U.: The performance of TCP/IP for networks with high bandwidth-delay products and random loss. IEEE/ACM Trans. Netw. **5**(3), 336–350 (1997)
21. Merkel, D.: Docker: lightweight linux containers for consistent development and deployment. Linux J. **2014**(239), 2 (2014)
22. Nah, F.F.-H.: A study on tolerable waiting time: how long are web users willing to wait? Behav. Inf. Technol. **23**(3), 153–163 (2004)
23. Papakos, P., Capra, L., Rosenblum, D.S.: VOLARE: Context-aware adaptive cloud service discovery for mobile systems. In: Proceedings of the 9th International Workshop on Adaptive and Reflective Middleware, ARM 2010, pp. 32–38. ACM (2010)
24. Petcu, D., Di Nitto, E., Ardagna, D., Solberg, A., Casale, G.: Towards multi-clouds engineering. In: 2014 IEEE Conference on Computer Communications Workshops (INFOCOM WKSHPS), April 2014
25. Popa, L., Ghodsi, A., Stoica, I.: HTTP as the narrow waist of the future internet. In: Proceedings of the 9th ACM SIGCOMM Workshop on Hot Topics in Networks, Hotnets-IX, pp. 6:1–6:6. ACM (2010)
26. Samreen, F., Blair, G.S., Rowe, M.: Adaptive decision making in multi-cloud management. In: Proceedings of the CrossCloud Brokers International Workshop, pp. 4:1–4:6. ACM, December 2014
27. Sat, B., Wah, B.W.: Analyzing voice quality in popular VoIP applications. IEEE Multimed. **16**(1), 46–59 (2009)
28. Semke, J., Mahdavi, J., Mathis, M.: Automatic TCP buffer tuning. ACM SIGCOMM Comput. Commun. Rev. **28**(4), 315–323 (1998)
29. Soltesz, S., Pötzl, H., Fiuczynski, M.E., Bavier, A., Peterson, L.: Container-based operating system virtualization: a scalable, high-performance alternative to hypervisors. ACM SIGOPS Operating Syst. Rev. **41**(3), 275–287 (2007)
30. Tyson, G., Kaune, S., Miles, S., Elkhatib, Y., Mauthe, A., Taweel, A.: A trace-driven analysis of caching in content-centric networks. In: Proceedings of the 21st International Conference on Computer Communications and Networks (ICCCN 2012). IEEE, August 2012
31. Tyson, G., Sastry, N., Rimac, I., Cuevas, R., Mauthe, A.: A survey of mobility in information-centric networks: Challenges and research directions. In: Proceedings of the 1st ACM Workshop on Emerging Name-Oriented Mobile Networking Design - Architecture, Algorithms, and Applications, NoM 2012, pp. 1–6. ACM (2012)
32. Vanbrabant, B., Joosen, W.: Configuration management as a multi-cloud enabler. In: Proceedings of the CrossCloud Brokers International Workshop, pp. 1:1–1:3. ACM, December 2014
33. Weigle, E., chun Feng, W.: A comparison of TCP automatic tuning techniques for distributed computing. In: Proceedings of the IEEE HPDC, pp. 265–272 (2002)
34. Winstein, K., Balakrishnan, H.: TCP ex machina: Computer-generated congestion control. ACM SIGCOMM Comput. Commun. Rev. **43**(4), 123–134 (2013)
35. Zhu, L., Xu, D., Xu, X.S., Tran, A.B., Weber, I., Bass, L.: Challenges in practicing high frequency releases in cloud environments. In: Secnd International Workshop on Release Engineering, Mountain View, USA, pp. 21–24, April 2014

Agent Knowledge and Beliefs in a Cloud

N.V. Shilov[1,2]($\boxtimes$)

[1] A.P. Ershov Institute of Informatics Systems,
Lavren'ev avenue, 6, Novosibirsk, Russia
[2] Nazarbayev University, Kabanbay Batyr avenue, 53, Astana, Kazakhstan
shilov@iis.nsk.su, nikolay.shilov@nu.edu.kz

Abstract. Cloud computing is a concept that is in use since late 2000s related to consumption of distributed computer resources, namely servers and networks for data storage and access. In the paper we examine knowledge-based algorithms for agents that have access to a resource center to use some of available discrete resources. We assume that resource items are passive, they form a cloud, any item can be lend on demand to any agent if and only if there is no races for this item with other agents. All agents are rational and can communicate with each other in P2P-manner, negotiate, flip and swap (change intentions) so that all flips/swaps always must be rational for participating agents. The problem is to design a multiagent algorithm, which allows each agent sooner or later to access some resource item. We present a uniform algorithm scheme and then specialize for the following particular problems: *Robots in Space* and *Rational Agents at the Marketplace*.

1 Introduction

The issues of *trust aspects* (functional correctness, safety, security, reliability, credibility, usability) in multi-agent systems have received a lot of attention. Methods to guarantee functional correctness, safety, and security as well as techniques to ensure reliability in distributed, self-organizing systems are under investigation by different research communities and (in particular) in a multiagent research paradigm.

In general, a paradigm is an approach to the formulation (formalization) of problems and the ways to solve them. The term comes from Greek and means pattern, example. A contemporary meaning of science paradigm is due to well-known book [10] by T. Kuhn. Robert Floyd was the first who had explicitly used the term paradigm in the Computer Science context in his Turing Award Lecture in 1978.

Multiagent paradigm is a common name for several related research and development approaches in Computer Science, in Artificial Intelligence, Information Systems, etc. In this paper we are bound to Computer Science multiagent paradigm as sketched below.

The research has been supported by Russian Foundation for Basic Research (grant 13-01-00643-a).

R. Horne (Ed.): EGC 2015, CCIS 514, pp. 11–20, 2015.
DOI: 10.1007/978-3-319-25043-4_2

A *distributed system* consists of multiple autonomous "computers" (programs with distributed memory) that communicate through a network [20]. A *multi-agent system* is a distributed system that consists of asynchronous (*rational*) *agents*. An agent is an autonomous reactive and projective *object* (in OO-sense) whose internal states may be characterized in terms of *Beliefs* (B), *Desires* (D), and *Intentions* (I). (Agents of the described kind are usually called BDI-agents [22].) A rational agent has clear "preferences" and always chooses the action (in feasible actions) that leads to the "best" outcome for itself; in contrast, a bounded rationality is "decision making" limited by the cognitive and deductive abilities of agents or other constrains (e.g. amount of time they have to make decisions). A *multiagent algorithm* is a distributed algorithm (protocol) [21] that solves some problem by means of cooperative work of agents in a multiagent system.

Agent's beliefs represent its ideas and opinions about itself, other agents, and the network; these ideas and opinions may be incomplete, inconsistent, and (even) incorrect in contrast to agent *knowledge*. We distinguish belief and knowledge notions according to the famous Plato thesis: *Knowledge is true belief.* Thus our approach to *knowledge* and *belief* is not very formal like in [6], but (we demonstrate in the paper that) it can be formalized in terms of *interpreted systems* [4,11,19].

Agent's desires represent its long-term aims, obligations and purposes (that may be controversial). Agent's intension is its plan how to implement its desires or a short-term individual planning. *Reactivity* means that every agent could change its beliefs, desires, and intentions after communication and interaction with other agents (the *environment*). (In particular, some former beliefs may transfer to knowledge about the environment, some may be refuted.) *Projectivity* is agent's ability to design/modify/adopt short-term plans (i.e. its intentions) according to updated information about the environment.

Some other notions related to multiagent systems are defined below. A *autonomous* agent changes its personal beliefs, desires and intentions by its own reasons, the change can't be decreed by any other agent. A *rational* agent has clear preferences and always chooses the action (in feasible actions) that leads to the best outcome for itself; a *bounded rationality* is decision making (basically planning) limited by the cognitive abilities of agents (e.g. the finite amount of time they have to make decisions) [14]. Agent's *privacy* is an opportunity to hide in negotiations data that the agent supposes to be private. [5,7]; in contrast, agent's *anonymity* is its opportunity not to revile its identity in negotiations.

In this paper we study multiagent algorithms (protocols for multiagent systems) for solving instances of the following general problem that we call *Discreet Resources Allocation Problem* (DRAP):

> There is a cloud of discreet resources consisting of a fix number of items (or pieces that are not dividable any more); there are also rational agents, each of which pretends for individual exclusive access to an item (exactly one); all agents can communicate and negotiate in peer-to-peer manner; the problem is to define a belief- and rationality-based protocol of

pairwise communications and negotiations, virtual flips/swaps of intentions (i.e. items) between agents, a protocol that eventually leads every agent to the knowledge about the individual resource item that belongs to the agent; it will be an advantage if the resulting global resource allocation will meet some global optimality criterion.

One can argue that DRAP can be solved by distributed *consensus* or *leader election* algorithms [3]. It is true in a distributed paradigm, but not in the multiagent paradigm, because sharing of private data is very legal in distributed systems, but not in multiagent systems. In particular, it is possible to elect a leader, pass it agents' private data, then let the leader to assign individual resource items to all agents according to some global optimality criterion. But agents in that distributed algorithm are too passive in problem solving and they send too much individual data to the leader. More over, in multiagent paradigm every agent (including the leader) should care just about itself (i.e. its individual knowledge about its individual safety and its individual resource item), but not about other agents and the system.

Doctoral Dissertation [12] gives a general survey of the Distributed Resource Allocation Problem in a frame of agent-based approach. Using standard terminology we could distinguish the following features of our approach to the problem.

– Resources are discreet, not dividable, not sharable, static, single-unit.
– Agents have quantitative preference structure, i.e. agents' utility function maps numbers to a set of resources.
– Resource allocations are evaluated by the utilitarian welfare which is the sum of individual utilities.
– Our multi-agent systems handle homogeneous populations, where all agents act according to the same behavior scenario.
– The social graph (i.e. agents' communication graph) is complete: everybody can talk with everyone.
– Any time each agent knows its own intention, but never the hole intentions of all other agents.
– We use bilateral swap transactions (which involve only two agents at a time) and individual flips.

In addition our algorithms are knowledge- and rational-based, privacy-preserving but not anonymous (i.e. agents need to revile their identity).

The rest of the paper is organized as follows. In the next Sect. 2 we introduce and discus particular examples of DRAP. Then, in Sect. 3, we present and discuss the algorithm for DRAP and how to specialise it for two paerticular instances of DRAP (from Sect. 2). In the concluding Sect. 4 we discuss relations of the presented research to so called *social computing* [1] and/or *social software* [13].

2   DRAP Special Cases

2.1   RinS: Robots in a Space

RinS problem formulated below is a multidimensional generalization of *Mars Robot Puzzle* (MRP) that has been studied in [2,17]: MRP is just RinS in 2-dimensional Euclidian space.

> There are $n > 0$ autonomous robots and the same number of shelters in a general position in a Euclidean space. A position of every shelter is fixed and known to every robot. Every robot knows about existence of all other robots, but does not know their locations. Robots can communicate in peer-to-peer manner only. At some moment each robot stops and fixes its current position. Then every robot should choose a shelter to move in by a straight way. Robots should not collide. The problem: Design a multiagent algorithm that guarantees that every robot will eventually know an individual shelter such that its straight route to the selected shelter never intersects with straight routes of other robots.

We would like to point out that RinS and MRP are related to Multi-Agent Programming Contest (MAPC, http://multiagentcontest.org). In 2011 organizers of MAPC *began the fourth phase with the definition of a new scenario: "Agents on Mars". The goal is to implement a team of cooperating agents with different roles in order to occupy zones on planet Mars. The challenge of the scenario is its increased complexity, that is that we have defined 5 roles of agents with different properties and capabilities.* But the difference between RinS/MRP and MAPC is crucial: we care about straight routes and formal correctness.

2.2   RAM: Rational Agents at the Marketplace

RAM problem formulated below has been discussed first in [18].

> At the Marketplace there are $n > 0$ buyers and $m \geq n$ salesman. Every salesman sells a (single) unit of some indivisible good ("a piece of cake") by individual prices for different buyers. Salesmen are passive: they do not care if their goods are sold out and who buy the goods. But every buyer is rational: it has to purchase exactly one unit of goods and it knows its individual prices from every salesman. Buyers can choose and flip salesmen, negotiate pairwise, swap salesmen in pairs, make price concessions. But every above action should benefit a buyer. A buyer can make a deal with a salesman iff it knows that nobody pretends for a deal with this salesman. The problem: Design a multiagent algorithm for buyers which guarantees that every buyer eventually buy something.

The difference between RAM and RinS/MRP is manyfold. First, in RAM agents are assumed to be rational, while in MRP agents do not care about their benefits (preferences) at all. Next, MRP has a clear geometric interpretation, but it is not clear from the very beginning, whether any intersection-free set (of routes) exists, and, hence it is not obvious that a desired protocol may exist. Fortunately, the existence of these routes could be proved by contradiction, or by reduction to the *assignment problem* in Graph Theory, or to the convex hull problem in Combinatorial Geometry.

The RAM problem is related to the classic *Cake Cutting Problem* (CC-problem, also known as *Fair Division Problem*) that has been introduced by a group of Polish mathematicians, H. Steinhaus, B. Knaster and S. Banach [1]. The CC-problem is to divide an infinitely dividable resource ("cake") in such a way that all recipients believe that they have received a fair amount. A special cases of the problem are *proportional* and *envy-free* division. Differences between RAM and CC-problem are evident: in CC-problem a cake is an infinitely dividable resource, while in RAM-problem a "resource" has been cut already; solutions of the CC-problem may be sequential, while solutions (if any) of RAM must be multiagent (i.e. distributed, parallel and concurrent) by the problem statement.

At the same time RAM problem is also closely related to the following *Stable Marriage Problem* (SMP) [9]. Given n men and n women, where each person has ranked all members of the opposite sex with a unique number between 1 and n in order of preference, marry the men and women together such that there are no two people of opposite sex who would both rather have each other than their current partners. (If there are no such pairs, all the marriages are said to be stable.) A non-deterministic but centralized and sequential algorithm has been developed by D. Gale and L. Shapley for SMP [9]. It makes the difference between SMP and RAM: SMP implicitly assumes a single sequential matchmaker, while RAM explicitly states that the problem must be solved by agents themselves.

2.3   RaceP: Race for Processors

The following new problem is closely related to DARP but is not a special case of the problem due to *dynamics* of arriving and served processes.

> There is a resource center consisting of (1) $n > 0$ (different) processors, (2) a pool with $m > 0$ tasks, and (3) a monitor for processor's load and a state of the processers. The monitor have marked all tasks in the pool by a time stamp upon their arrival (into the pool); assigns instantly a free processor to some task, if the task requests the processor; removes assigned tasks from the pool, and returns processors to the center after task execution. Every task is an agent, that knows an individual "wanted" process. The problem: Design a multiagent algorithm for tasks which guarantees that every task in the pool eventually be assigned by a processor to be performed.

3   Algorithm and Correctness

An *unified* multiagent algorithm SOpt (*Search of Optimum*) for DRAP is presented below in this section. It is a generalization of SMEx-algorithm [2,17] that solves MRP. Correctness of specialized algorithms for RinS/MRP and RAM problems have been proved in [2,17], but its adjustment for RaceP is still an open question. The correctness proofs follow main steps and are similar to the proof of SMEx algorithm. Both protocols SMEx and SOpt rely upon the following fairness communication assumption [17]: communication (in a multiagent system) is said to be *fair*, if every agent which would like to communicate with any other agent will communicate eventually. Fairness has been discussed in [8].

Algorithm SOpt for an individual agent can be described informally as follows. Any time every agent can ask a monitor about the set of *Agents* that currently compete for resources. At every moment every agent has some particular resource item as its current intention; at the very beginning this intention is defined by function $INI : Agents \rightarrow Resources$. Conflicts between agents can be checked by predicate $Conf : Agents \times Resources \times Agents \times Resources \rightarrow Boolean$ such that for all agents $i \neq j$, for all resource items u_i and u_j, $Conf(i, u_i, j, u_j) \Leftrightarrow Conf(j, u_j, i, u_i)$. Beliefs of every agent are represented by several integer counters:

- NC for *Number of Conflicts* is used by instant and time agents,
- CF for *Conflict-Free* agents is used by time agents only.

We distinguish also *instant* and *time* agents: the former agent can catch (or grab) the allocated piece immediately and instantly, the latter needs some time to catch the allocated piece: an instant agent grabs its resource instantly as soon $NC = 0$, while a time agent waits for all other agents, since acquiring of the resource needs time (during which a new conflict may occur). NC represents agent's upper estimation of number of agents with whom it may have conflict, and, respectively, CF represents its lower estimation of number of agents that have no conflicts at all. In particular,

- the agent believes that it does not conflict with any other agent as soon as $NC = 0$;
- the agent believes that there is no conflicts in the system as soon as $NC = 0$ and $CF = 2 \times (n - 1)$, i.e. it believes that it has no rivals, and it checks *twice* that all other agents believe that they do not have conflicts also.

But in the case when two agents have a conflict, then they resolve the trouble by non-deterministic function $Sol : Agents \times Resources \times Agents \times Resources \rightarrow Resources$ such that for all agents $i \neq j$, for all resource units u_i and u_j, if $Conf(i, u_i, j, u_j)$ then $Sol(i, u_i, j, u_j)$ and $Sol(j, u_j, i, u_i)$ are different resource unites.

Pseudocode of the SOpt-algorithm follows, but first we would like to comment a meaning of some variables: Me is a variable for personal agent's identification number; cur_un and par_un are the variables for intentions of the agent and its partner (i.e. for resource items); par_bel is a variable for partner's belief that the partner is conflict-free; contacts is a variable for a set of agents. (The algorithm is given for time agents. Please, ignore all instances of CF counter for instant agents.)

```
algorithm SOpt::
const Me: integer in [1..n]
var NC: integer in [1..(n-1)];
var CF: integer in [1..(n-1)];
var contacts: set of [1..n];
var partner: integer in [1..n];
var cur_un, par_un: integer in [1..n];
var par_bel: boolean;
begin
1:   NC:= (n - 1); CF:= 0;
2:   cur_un: = INI(Me);
3:   repeat
4:    if NC > 0 then NC:= (n - 1);
5:    contacts:= Agents \{Me};
6:     repeat
7:      partner: = any agent in the contacts ready to communicate¹;
8:      start communication session with the partner:
9:      { send (<cur_un>;<(NC=0)?>) to partner ||
10:        receive (<par_un>;<par_bel>) from partner}
11:     if Conf(Me, cur_un, partner, par_unit) then
12:       {cur_un:= Sol(Me, cur_un, partner, par_un);
13:         NC:= (n - 1); CF:= 0}
14:     else if NC > 0
15:          then {NC:= (NC - 1); CF:= 0}
16:          else if par_bel
17:              then CF:= CF + 1
18:              else {NC:= (n - 1); CF:= 0}
19:     close communication session with partner;
20:    contacts:= remove partner from contacts;
21:    until contacts becomes empty
22: until (NC = 0  ∧  CF = 2×(n - 1))
end.
```

Proposition 1. *If a multiagent system consists of a fair communication scheduler and agents that all execute SOpt protocol, and system terminates, then all agents will know their conflict-free pieces of the resource upon the termination.*

A *well-founded set* is a partial order $(D, \leq)$ without infinite (strictly) decreasing sequences. Let us say that a distributed system is well-founded, if there exists a well-founded set $(D, \leq)$ and a *well-mapping* F from system configurations (i.e. its global states) into D such that for all agents $i \neq j$, for all resource units u_i and u_j, $Conf(i, u_i, j, u_j)$ implies that execution of $Sol(i, u_i, j, u_j)$ and $Sol(j, u_j, i, u_i)$ in any order reduces the value of F.

---

¹ A scheduler resolves this request.

Proposition 2. *If a multiagent system consists of a fair communication scheduler and agents that all execute SOpt protocol, and the system is well-founded then the system eventually terminates.*

The specialization of above general algorithm for the particular problems RinS and RAM consists in a manner of recognizing and resolving conflicts. In case of RinS

- predicate *Conf* is true iff routes of robots intersects,
- function *Sol* swaps shelters for robots, and
- well-mapping F maps system configurations into the sum of all distances from robots to shelters.

In case of RAM

- predicate *Conf* is true iff there is a competition of buyers for the same salesman,
- function *Sol* implements a game with better price as a gain, and
- well-mapping F maps system configurations into a total price for all goods.

4   Conclusion

4.1   Summary

In the paper we discussed multiagent approach to the discrete resource allocation problem (DRAP), presented a multiagent algorithm that solves the problem under assumption of communication fairness and well-foundness, and presented particular examples of problems that can be solved on base of the our results.

We also have to remark that we considered very idealistic multiagent systems that consists of absolutely reliable (non-faulty) agents in a static situation. Hence a topic for further research may be study of more realistic case of faulty agents and dynamic systems. Anonymity could be studied also, since our SOpt algorithm requires from agents to inform partners about their identity.

There exist sophisticated distributed algorithms for resource allocation problem, but *formal* functional correctness and etc. usually is out of scope of these works. In contrast, a contribution of our paper is to study of this aspect (although for idealized examples). We have to mention in this extended abstract that our correctness proof is manual. But one can observe that the formal description of the interpreted system for DRAP makes possible to verify the algorithm automatically with aid of techniques developed in [16]. It will be a topic for further research also.

4.2   Cloud vs. Crowd

We have mentioned in Sect. 2 that Ratioanl Agents at Marketplace (RAM) problem is closely related to the classic Cake Cutting Problem (CC-problem) and discussed similarity and differences between these two problems. But in spite of these differences, RAM and CC problems have something in common since they both are examples of a new research paradigm of that is called *social computing* or *social software* [1,13]. The essence of this paradigm is sketched in the next paragraph.

In the modern world very many social requirements and procedures have algorithmic character. These requirements can be written as (semi-)formal specifications and procedures — software (in a pseudo-code). Then the properties of these procedures can be analyzed and verified by formal methods. Well, the results of the formal analysis or verification may be interpreted in socially significant terms. And though about social computing/software started talking only in a XXI century, but it is possible to consider as the first example of application of this paradigm research of the Cake Cutting Problem by H. Shteinhaus, B. Knaster and S. Banach.

In particular, Rational Agents at Marketplace can be considered as an example of social computing/software research [15]. In social computing/software paradigm "crowd" with communication network and access to resources may be considered as agents and cloud of resources. But in this context study of efficiency, fairness, privacy and anonymity of multiagent algorithms get much more importance than in this paper.

References

1. Brams, S.J., Taylor, A.T.: Fair Division - From Cake-Cutting to Dispute Resolution. Cambridge University Press, Cambridge (1996)
2. Bodin, E.V., Garanina, N.O., Shilov, N.V., Mars, N.V.: Robot puzzle (a multiagent approach to the Dijkstra problem). Model. Anal. Inf. Syst. **18**(2), 113–128 (2011). (in Russian)
3. Cachin, C., Guerraoui, L.S.: Rodrigues Introduction to Reliable and Secure Distributed Programming, 2nd edn. Springer, New York (2011)
4. Fagin, R., Halpern, J.Y., Moses, Y., Vardi, M.Y.: Reasoning About Knowledge. MIT Press, Cambridge (1995)
5. Halpern, J., O'Neill, K.: Anonymity and information hiding in multiagent systems. J. Comput. Secur. **13**(3), 483–514 (2005)
6. Hintikka, J.: Knowledge and Belief. Cornell University Press, Ithaca (1962)
7. Hughes, D., Shmatikov, V.: Information hiding, anonymity and privacy: a modular approach. J. Comput. Secur. **12**(1), 3–36 (2004)
8. de Jong, S., Tuyls, K., Verbeeck, K.: Fairness in multiagent systems. Knowl. Eng. Rev. **23**(2), 153–180 (2008)
9. Knuth, D.E.: Stable Marriage and its Relation to Other Combinatorial Problems. CRM Proceedings and Lecture Notes, vol. 10. American Mathematical Society, Providence (1997)
10. Kuhn, T.S.: The Structure of Scientific Revolutions, 3rd edn. University of Chicago Press, Chicago (1996)
11. Lomuscio, A., Ryan, M.D.: On the relation between interpreted systems and Kripke models. In: Wobcke, W., Pagnucco, M., Zhang, C. (eds.) Agents and Multi-Agent Systems Formalisms, Methodologies, and Applications. LNCS (LNAI), vol. 1441, pp. 46–59. Springer, Heidelberg (1997)

12. Nongaillard, A.: An Agent-Based Approach for Distributed Resource Allocations. Doctoral dissertation. Concordia University Montreal, Canada (2009)
13. Parikh, R.: Social software. Synthese **132**, 187–211 (2002)
14. Russell, S.J., Norvig, P.: Artificial Intelligence: A Modern Approach, 3rd edn. Prentice Hall, Saddle River (2010)
15. Satekbayeva, A., Shilov, N.V.: Some results on multiagent algorithms in social computing/software context. Information **17**(1), 229–240 (2014)
16. Shilov, N.V., Garanina, N.O., Choe, K.-M.: Update and abstraction in model checking of knowledge and branching time. Fundameta Informaticae **72**(1–3), 347–361 (2006)
17. Shilov, N.V., Garanina, N.O., Bodin, E.V.: Multiagent approach to a Dijkstra problem. In: Proceedings of Workshop on Concurrency, Specification, and Programming CS&P 2010, pp. 73–84. Humboldt-Universität zu, Berlin (2010)
18. Shilov, N.V., Garanina, N.O.: Rational agents at the marketplace. In: Proceedings of Workshop on Concurrency, Specification and Programming CS&P 2011, pp. 465–476. Bialystok University of Technology, Pułtusk, Poland, 28–30 September 2011
19. Su, K., Luo, X., Sattar, A., Orgun, M.A.: The interpreted system model of knowledge, belief, desire and intention. In: Proceedings of the Fifth International Joint Conference on Autonomous Agents and Multiagent Systems (AAMAS 2006), pp. 220–222 (2006)
20. Tanenbaum, A.S., Van Steen, M.: Distributed Systems: Principles and Paradigms, 2nd edn. Prentice Hall, Saddle River (2007)
21. Tel, G.: Introduction to Distributed Algorithms, 2nd edn. Cambridge University Press, Cambridge (2000)
22. Wooldridge, M.: An Introduction to Multiagent Systems. Jhon Willey & Sons, Chichester (2002)

Could We Fit the Internet in a Box?

Gareth Tyson[1(✉)] , Arjuna Sathiaseelan[2], and Jörg Ott[3]

[1] Queen Mary University of London, London, UK
g.tyson@qmul.ac.uk
[2] University of Cambridge, Cambridge, UK
[3] Aalto University, Espoo, Finland

Abstract. It is estimated that only 40 % of the world's households are connected to the Internet. Half of them are in less developed countries, where household Internet penetration has only reached 28 %. This is in stark contrast to the 78 % of households in more developed countries. A key challenge facing the next generation is therefore enabling wider participation in the Internet, as well as the benefits it brings. This paper explores the feasibility of capturing network applications and services in a single locally usable "Internet Box". The Box will operate independently from the rest of the Internet, allowing those without traditional connectivity to use the "Internet" in an simulated and disconnected manner. We conclude that the concepts have great potential, and explore some of the remaining challenges, as well as milestones achieved in the literature so far.

1 Introduction

It is estimated that only 37.9 % of the world's population have Internet access [1]. In developing countries, this value is only 29.9 %, in stark contrast to 75.7 % in the developed world. The economic benefits of Internet access are also disproportionately biased, with developed economies ahead by a factor of 25 % [2]. Despite this, remarkably, even some wealthy countries suffer from similar problems; in New Orleans, for example, the poorer wards have broadband subscription rates between only 0 and 40 %. A key challenge facing the next generation is therefore enabling wider participation in the Internet, as well as the benefits it brings. Before facing this challenge, it is first necessary to ask one question: What is the Internet? If you ask network engineers, they would explain the many details of TCP/IP. However, the everyday person might likely respond with services available via the Internet such as Google, Facebook, Twitter or Netflix. Hence, we argue that users want access to services — they are not concerned about how they are delivered.

The above observation is a powerful one because it relaxes some of the constraints on deploying the "Internet" to new regions. Specifically, we explore the feasibility of capturing network applications and services in a single locally usable box which we call the "Internet Box". The Box will operate independently from the rest of the Internet, allowing those without traditional connectivity to use the

© Springer International Publishing Switzerland 2015
R. Horne (Ed.): EGC 2015, CCIS 514, pp. 21–30, 2015.
DOI: 10.1007/978-3-319-25043-4_3

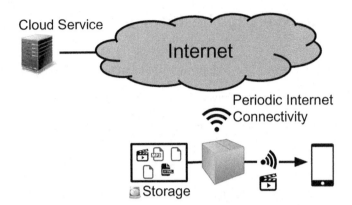

Fig. 1. Overview of the Box. A smartphone connects the the Box and requests a video that is transferred via WiFi. The film is locally stored on the Box and is therefore provided regardless of backhaul Internet connectivity. The Box may also have periodic Internet connectivity, allowing it to communicate with remote cloud services that can provide updated content.

"Internet" in an simulated and even (partly) disconnected manner. For example, locally caching a copy of a map on the Box would allow a user to access it regardless of the backhaul availability. This is shown in Fig. 1, where a user connects to the local Box via WiFi to download a video, which is locally stored.

Beyond this, there might be periodic backhaul connectivity to cloud service(s) that can provide fresh content when available. Advanced models could be built to make this process automatic. For instance, predictive algorithms could be developed to predict the content that will be requested from the Box in the future. Such algorithms could be executed whenever the Box achieves connectivity with the wider Internet. Through this, all future required resources could be pushed or pre-fetched and stored in the Box in anticipation of their usage.[1] If these principles are proven feasible, many localities that possess no connectivity could hopefully start to use Internet services immediately. The paper explores why this is a positive first step towards global access for all.

Recent efforts towards an Internet Box have already resulted in deployments. Most prominently, a project actually named "Internet in a Box" has had multiple successful deployments [4]. Such projects, however, face a number of challenges. An obvious problem that emerges is the inevitable lack of resources available in such environments. Storage and local network limitations, alongside poor backhaul connectivity, can result in many users being frustrated with the service they receive. Traditionally, such problems would be dealt with via typical "fair share" algorithms that operate agnostic to the higher level applications

---

[1] Flavours of this idea were suggested for connecting users accessing the Internet via satellite, e.g. to save capacity of satellite channels when serving the same content to many users [3] and for intermittently connected users (c.f. http://www.gedanken.org.uk/software/wwwoffle/).

(e.g. TCP congestion control). However, with extremely limited resources, these fair share algorithms can result in everybody receiving a unusable quality of service (much like experienced during past congestion collapse events [5]). Similarly, existing Box implementations operate in very constrained ways, generally just providing static content. The "Web 2.0" revolution has proven that this limitation is not long-term viable and, therefore, we also argue that the Box should be equipped with local services (e.g. social networks, picture sharing) that can be accessed by citizens.

This paper explores the potential of deploying a Box possessing local storage and computation into areas that have very limited Internet access (e.g. rural villages). Section 2 surveys related work in the area and highlights milestone implementations and deployments of these principles so far. Section 3 details the key system components that must exist within the box to correctly operate. We explore how the Box might be implemented and used in Sect. 4. Finally, in Sect. 5, we conclude the paper, highlighting further interesting avenues of work.

2   Background and Related Work

Recent years have witnessed several projects that propose concepts related to an Internet Box. Most prominent is the aptly named Internet in a Box initiative [4]. This is a small networked device that is pre-loaded with curated content, e.g. books, Wikipedia. The box is enabled with local WiFi connectivity, allowing users to connect and access the locally stored content. A similar approach is taken by Liberouter [6], which offers access to generic content that might be of interest to a given neighbourhood. A common use case is exploiting this type of equipment for learning purposes. The Open Learning Toolkit [7] is one such example; it exposes an HTML5 interface to allow learners (generally school children) to access various resources such as textbooks. It can operate in both connected and disconnected modes, the former allowing new content to be fetched. Other closely related systems include The Library For All [8], and the Library Box [9].

An alternative to disconnected devices is Outernet [10], which takes a unique approach to content delivery. Rather than following the Internet's usual request-response model, where a client (e.g. the Box) requests content, Outernet *broadcasts* content via Satellite. Any Boxes within range, will therefore passively receive new bundles of content (much like a TV receives broadcast signals). Recent work has also explored the possibility of using 4G broadcast signals for similar aims [11]. Preliminary evaluations of this concept have been very positive; in [11], the authors found that a 100 MB broadcast of content could preempt upto 40 % of requests. Work has also been performed into pre-fetching particular types of content; for example, SCORE [12] predicts users' catch-up video consumption patterns and automatically records videos from TV broadcast signals, rather than leaving the user to fetch content over IP (thereby saving energy and network overheads). A key enabler to these technologies is past measurement studies that have explored how users access the Internet. There have been a handful of studies into how people in developing regions use the Internet (e.g. which services they access). Most noteworthy is Johnson *et al.*;

the authors inspected a two month network trace in Zambia; this, amongst other things, showed the impact of traffic from content-heavy peer-to-peer systems. They used this insight to design VillageShare, which operates as a time-delayed proxy for use in rural villages.

There are a number of remaining technical challenges that needs to be addressed in this domain. There are obviously key hardware issues that must be faced, particularly relating to energy management and cost. Building reliable devices at affordable prices (that can be deployed in developing regions) is not trivial. This is exacerbated by the fact that environments are often quite severe, where devices may be exposed to extreme weather (e.g. very high or low temperatures). Another huge challenge is the loading of appropriate content onto the Box. In existing projects, this is generally done in a relatively manual way, whereby content is curated and selected by an appropriate party. There are techniques for citizens to request specific content, but this is often cumbersome. For example, the Outernet allows users to request content be added to the storage by SMS. As such, it would be much better if this could be an automated process, where the Box learnt and automatically loaded "optimal" content for its locale. In either case, it is likely that some users would be disappointed by the choices made, leading to the need for interaction between users and the Box to find a compromise (c.f. interactive web caching [13]).

Another key limitation of existing solutions is their lack of support for dynamic services. Whereas it is relatively easy to load a Box with static content, it is much more difficult to host and execute services. The benefits of achieving this goal are significant. It would allow developers (both local and global) to instantiate beneficial services that could perform tasks far beyond simple content provision. A classic example would be to introduce a local social networking services that allows people to share photos etc. There are many conceivable services that could be used for more practical purposes too. For instance, a crop disease diagnosis service could be provided that allow farmers to upload pictures of diseased crops; these could then be automatically analysed to return treatment advice. Although deploying services like this into edge networks has yet to become mainstream, new technologies (e.g. unikernels [14] or service-centric networks [15]) makes this increasingly possible.

Of course, all the above concepts further depend on one thing: Being able to transport content and/or services from the source to the Box post-deployment. Without such a capability, the Box would forever remain at its factory default. A key challenge is therefore finding and exploiting (intermittent) low cost backhaul connectivity. This would most likely be occasional satellite communications, broadcast-style delivery and/or the ability to periodiccally move the Box to an area that has connectivity. A closely related topic to this is that of delay-tolerant networks (DTNs). A DTN is a type of network that supports the existence of significant delays or disruptions between sending and receiving parties [16]. Specifically, DTNs propose a store-and-forward architecture in which data units, termed *bundles*, can be temporarily stored at nodes (during network disruptions) until an appropriate next hop can be found [17]. Traditionally, these disruptions and delays could be caused by long distances (e.g. interstellar communications

[18]) or, alternatively, by network partitions. The latter is the case for the Box as, in essence, the Box operates as a disconnected component of the network. These principles were made available, for example, in the KioskNet project [19], which introduced boxes into known small kiosks. Passing vehicles (e.g. buses) would then carry content and load it into the kiosks as they drove past.

Another closely related concept is that of information-centric networks (ICNs). An ICN is a network with the sole purpose of delivering content [20–22]. As such, an ICN exposes a publish/subscribe style abstraction unlike the existing Socket API [23]. This is because a host-centric network (HCN) is designed to scalably route packets from a source to a destination, whilst an ICN is designed to scalably deliver content from providers to consumers. This is clearly a technology that maps closely to the Box, which primarily is oriented towards the delivery of content. Prominent examples of ICNs include DONA [24], PURSUIT [21], Named Data Networking (NDN) [20] and Juno [25]. We believe that these principles combined (ICN and DTN) could offer a strong foundation to build Box technology. This could then be combined with emerging service-oriented technologies (e.g. Jitsu [14]) to allow a Box to run local services. Our past work has taken the first steps towards this by integrating ICN and DTN functionality [26]. A further overview of key scenarios and uses for ICN can be found here [27].

3   Strawman Requirements and Design

We next detail a strawman design of the Box, exploring key components that must be built. There are four architectural components; each constitute both hardware and software

3.1   Storage

To enable totally disconnected operation, it is necessary to maintain a significant amount of local storage in the Box. This allows popular objects (both content and services) to be served locally without needing to use any egress network connectivity. In the simplest case, this storage device could be pre-loaded with important content (e.g. Wikipedia, medical information) at the factory. Storage is a cheap commodity, with multi-TB drives available for ≈£50 (and below). This might constitute significant capital expenditure in a developing region, but it could be treated as a long-term investment for a community. Perhaps the most notable bottleneck is energy consumption. Mechanical disks, although cheap, consume large energy quantities due to the need for moving parts (although low energy mechanical storage disks are available). In contrast, Solid State Drives are much more energy efficient, although financial cost is greater.

Beyond these hardware considerations, it is clearly also necessary to build intelligent algorithms that can appropriately select what is stored. In situations where content and services are statically loaded at the factory, this is less important. However, if there is any level of content/service churn over time, this must be managed in an appropriate manner (more information is provided in Sect. 4). This is closely related to recent work on ICN caching [28], as well as work on pre-fetching, which aims to predict the content requests before they happen [12]. In these cases, the challenge would be to perfectly predict all requests by users so that they can be pre-emptively stored on the Box in advance.

3.2   Local Connectivity

Clearly, it is necessary to provide some mechanism by which citizens can gain access to the Box. The simplest approach would be to introduce a WiFi network interface. Of course, this assumes that users nearby own a device capable of connecting. This would be the case for all network alternatives, e.g. Bluetooth or wired Ethernet. A different approach would be to introduce some sort of user interface (touch screen) to the Box itself. On the one hand, this would make the box more self contained, however, on the other hand, it would limit the number of people who could simultaneously use it. Further, it would dramatically increase complexity, cost and energy consumption. As such, providing simple WiFi communications, that can be accessed using a low-cost tablet, would be preferential.

A further use of local connectivity would be to update the storage with fresh content. One possibility would be to use vehicles, which can carry content and transmit it to the box when they come into range (like KioskNet [19]). Alternatively, somebody could physically move the Box to an area that has fresh content to download. Of course, this would all require seamless mechanisms that automatically update the Box without human intervention (i.e. as soon a the Box comes into range of another content source).

3.3   Backhaul Connectivity

An optional addition to the Box would be a network interface that provides backhaul connectivity (i.e. wide area Internet communications). This would be highly desirable, as it would allow the box to refresh the content and services it stores without the need to move the box or to use a KioskNet-like mechanism. Unfortunately, the regions where the Box might be deployed are unlikely to easily support widescale communications at a low cost. Consequently, the box must be able to operate with and without Internet connectivity. Particularly, the Box should support on-off backhaul support, where connectivity is intermittent. By enabling all Box deployments with both capabilities, we also argue that this can more seamlessly allow citizens to transition to "real" Internet access when wide area connectivity is made available in a region.

3.4   Service Management

As previously stated, it would be beneficial if the Box could support functionality beyond static content storage. Running a small service platform within the

Box would allow things like local social networks and even games to be hosted. Obviously the capabilities of these would be limited by the resources of the Box and, therefore, service mangement in this context would be extremely important. Specifically, it would be necessary to build a platform that can securely host *very* lightweight services with the ability to individually control and limit their resource consumption (based on a range of requirements). These constraints mean that running large numbers of complex services would be difficult. Instead, specific techniques would be needed to strictly limit the operations of each service in a fair manner.

3.5   Remote Management

As stated above, the Box would be ill-suited to running and managing complex services and tasks locally. For example, deciding what to store on the Box could potentially involve complicated operations (compiling user histories, modelling their interests, predicting future request patterns, selecting a subset of content to request). Due to cost constraints, for some deployments, it would be undesirable to build the Box with sufficient memory and processing capacity to execute all these algorithms. It would therefore be desirable to be able to offload some of these tasks to remote execution (i.e. in a cloud). This could operate in a similar manner to CDroid [29] or ThinkAir [30] for mobile phones, where tasks are split between local and remote execution. Through this, the computational load on the Box could be reduced. Complexity in a disconnected scenario, however, is higher. For instance, the Box might not be able to communicate with the remote cloud service for an extended period. This would be particularly problematic if data must be kept up-to-date on both the Box and the cloud. As such, techniques must be developed to balance the need to offload computation with the limitations of the backahul communications availability.

4   Implementation Levels

There are several potential stages to the implementation. Currently, a small set of hardware systems have been built (e.g. [4]). The key challenge remaining is therefore devising means by which the resources of this hardware can be appropriately managed and extended to support more sophisticated behaviour (e.g. services). Here, we devise several key implementation steps for our future work:

1. The simplest implementation would be to provide a single Box that possesses static storage and local network connectivity. The Box would contain a large block of storage that is filled with curated static content (decided at the factory). Local WiFi would allow users to connect to the Box. Upon connection, users would be able to access a locally available portal that gives access to all content on the Box (e.g. via a web browser). In line with common usage, the most sensible portal might be a search engine interface with more structured access to content categories (similar to interactive web caching [13]).

2. The next implementation stage would extend the Box to support user uploaded content. This would allow users to create and share their own static media (e.g. webpages, videos). The uploaded content would then be integrated into the portal to make it locally available to all other users. Of course, this is accompanied by various audit, privacy and security challenges that would need addressing.

3. The next implementation stage would be to introduce active services onto the Box. This would move beyond static content provision. Potential services could be online social networks and voice communications. This would be limited to local interactions; for example, a social network service would only provide accounts for local users. Such services could be built over a uniker-nel platform like Jiitsu that allow extremely lightweight virtual machines to operate in resources constrained environments [14]; each service would exist as its own micro virtual machine that could be executed.

4. The next step would be to add one-way inbound communications to the Box. This is likely to be periodic and, potentially, unpredictable. This would allow the Box to receive one-way information from external parties. For example, this could involve satellite or radio broadcasts of fresh content/services (similar to Outernet [10]).

5. The next tier would introduce two-way communications. However, this will not necessarily be synchronous. Request/response intervals could be in the order of hours or days. Further, there may be extended periods without any connectivity whatsoever. This would allow information to be uploaded from the Box to third parties (e.g. offloaded cloud services).

6. Finally, the most advanced stage of implementation would be to add two-way synchronous connectivity. This would, in essence, provide full Internet connectivity to citizens, which is the final goal of our work.

5   Conclusion

This paper has explored a potential approach to deploying Internet-like services in areas that currently struggle to gain wide area connectivity. There are a number of challenges that remain. We therefore conclude with a brief summary of future issues to address. A particular problem is how such a Box could be filled with content and services. Currently, the predominant approach is through curated streams and content packages chosen by third parties. This raises a number of issues. It poses technical challenges, such as how dynamic shifts in content or service demand could be reacted to. Beyond this, it also raises ethical questions: Who is qualified to have control over what content should be accessible by a group of people? Making such as process transparent would not be trivial. Transporting content and services from the Internet onto the Box poses another key challenge. Clearly, this is straightforward if the Box is solely pre-loaded with content/services at the factory (i.e. there is no need to transport anything). However, if the Box is to be updated over time, it is necessary to execute algorithms that can decide what should be stored. A number of possibilities have been discussed in this paper, however, the most appropriate is not clear.

An open issue that we have not touched upon is that of commercialisation. It is likely many stakeholders (e.g. Box manufacturers, content providers) would need to monetise their "products" somehow. For example, how would content producers make money from uploading their content onto the Box? This is an issue that we leave for future exploration. However, to produce sustainable deployments, it is likely that this challenge must be faced.

It is important to finalise by saying that the purpose behind our work is *not* to create a two-tier Internet, in which certain people are limited to locally available content/services provided by the Box. Rather, it is intended as an intermediate step to better enable future deployments. Consequently, the nature of these future deployments must be considered. An obvious possibility is to introduce more sophisticated features to the Box, e.g. various novel services, that offer near identical support to the wider Internet. Of course, the next step beyond this would likely be to offer "real" Internet access, where the Box operates as a simple gateway (with a cache). An attractive property of the Box would be that by this point in time, people would have been given the opportunity to become familiar with the technology. Thus, the transition for local communications to global would be more seamless.

Acknowledgment. Arjuna Sathiaseelan and Jörg Ott were funded by the EC H2020 RIFE project, grant reference 644663

References

1. U. N. International Telecommunication Union (ITU), World telecommunication/ict indicators database (2013). http://www.itu.int/en/ITU-D/Statistics/Pages/stat/default.aspx
2. Strategy Dynamics Global SA, The emerging digital economy (2013). https://www.globaltrends.com/monthly-briefings/60-monthly-briefings/192-gt-briefing-june-2013-the-digital-economy
3. Rabinovich, M., Spatscheck, O.: Web caching and replication. Sigmod Rec. **32**(4), 107 (2003)
4. Internet in a box. http://internet-in-a-box.org/
5. Braden, B., Clark, D., Crowcroft, J., Davie, B., Deering, S., Estrin, D., Floyd, S., Jacobson, V., Minshall, G., Partridge, C., et al.: Recommendations on queue management and congestion avoidance in the internet (1998)
6. Karkkainen, T., Ott, J.: Liberouter: towards autonomous neighborhood networking. In: 2014 11th Annual Conference on Wireless On-demand Network Systems and Services (WONS), pp. 162–169. IEEE (2014)
7. Open learning toolkit. http://www.col.org/progServ/programmes/KM/Pages/Aptus.aspx
8. Library for all. https://www.libraryforall.org/
9. Library box. http://librarybox.us/
10. Outernet. https://www.outernet.is/en/
11. Finamore, A., Mellia, M., Gilani, Z., Papagiannaki, K., Erramilli, V., Grunenberger, Y.: Is there a case for mobile phone content pre-staging? In: Proceedings of the Ninth ACM Conference on Emerging Networking Experiments and Technologies, pp. 321–326. ACM (2013)

12. Nencioni, G., Sastry, N., Chandaria, J., Crowcroft, J.: Understanding and decreasing the network footprint of catch-up tv. In: Proceedings of the 22nd International Conference on WWW (2013)
13. Chen, J., Subramanian, L.: Interactive web caching for slow or intermittent networks. In: Proceedings of the 4th Annual Symposium on Computing for Development, p. 5. ACM (2013)
14. Madhavapeddy, A., Leonard, T., Skjegstad, M., et al.: Jitsu: Just-in-time summoning of unikernels. In: 12th USENIX Symposium on Networked System Design and Implementation (2015)
15. Braun, T., Hilt, V., Hofmann, M., Rimac, I., Steiner, M., Varvello, M.: Service-centric networking. In: 2011 IEEE International Conference on Communications Workshops (ICC), pp. 1–6. IEEE (2011)
16. Fall, K.: A delay-tolerant network architecture for challenged internets. In: Proceedings of SIGCOMM (2003)
17. Fall, K., Burleigh, S.: Bundle protocol specification. RFC 5206 (Experimental), November 2007
18. Burleigh, S., Hooke, A., Torgerson, L., Fall, K., Cerf, V., Durst, B., Scott, K., Weiss, H.: Delay-tolerant networking: an approach to interplanetary internet. Commun. Mag. IEEE **41**, 128–136 (2003)
19. Guo, S., Derakhshani, M., Falaki, M.H., Ismail, U., Luk, R., Oliver, E.A., Rahman, S.U., Seth, A., Zaharia, M.A., Keshav, S.: Design and implementation of the kioskNet system. Comput. Netw. **55**(1), 264–281 (2011)
20. Jacobson, V., Smetters, D.K., Thornton, J.D., Plass, M.F., Briggs, N.H., Braynard, R.L.: Networking named content. In: Proceedings 5th ACM CoNEXT (2009)
21. Trossen, D., Parisis, G.: Designing and realizing an information-centric internet. IEEE Commun. Mag. **50**, 60–67 (2012)
22. Kutscher, D., Farrell, S., Davies, E.: The NetInf Protocol. Internet Draft (2012)
23. Tyson, G., Mauthe, A., Kaune, S., Grace, P., Plagemann, T.: Juno: an adptive delivery-centric middleware. In: Proceedings 4th International Workshop on Future Media Networking (FMN) (2012)
24. Koponen, T., Chawla, M., Chun, B.-G., Ermolinskiy, A., Kim, K.H., Shenker, S., Stoica, I.: A data-oriented (and beyond) network architecture. SIGCOMM Comput. Commun. Rev. **37**(4), 181–192 (2007)
25. Tyson, G., Mauthe, A., Kaune, S., Grace, P., Taweel, A., Plagemann, T.: Juno: a middleware platform for supporting delivery-centric applications. ACM Trans. Internet Technol., vol. 12 (2012)
26. Tyson, G., Bigham, J., Bodanese, E.: Towards an information-centric delay-tolerant network. In: 2013 IEEE Conference on Computer Communications Workshops (INFOCOM WKSHPS), pp. 387–392. IEEE (2013)
27. Pentikousis, K., Ohlman, B., Corujo, D., et al.: Information centric networking: baseline scenarios, Technical report, ICNRG Internet-Draft (2014)
28. Tyson, G., Kaune, S., Miles, S., El-Khatib, Y., Mauthe, A., Taweel, A.: A trace-driven analysis of caching in content-centric networks. In: Proceedings International Conference on Computer Communication Networks (ICCCN) (2012)
29. Barbera, M., Kosta, S., Mei, A., Perta, V., Stefa, J.: Cdroid: towards a cloud-integrated mobile operating system. In: IEEE Conference on Computer Communications Workshops (INFOCOM WKSHPS), pp. 47–48. IEEE (2013)
30. Kosta, S., Aucinas, A., Hui, P., Mortier, R., Zhang, X.: Thinkair: dynamic resource allocation and parallel execution in the cloud for mobile code offloading. In: 2012 Proceedings IEEE INFOCOM, pp. 945–953. IEEE (2012)

Exemplified Study of WRED Algorithm Parameters Influence on IP-based Networks

Kuat Abdrau[1,2]([envelope])

[1] Faculty of Information Technology, Kazakh-British Technical University, Almaty, Kazakhstan

[2] Network Management Center, Kazakhtelecom, Almaty, Kazakhstan
kabdrau@gmail.com

Abstract. Within the TCP/IP model, if the transport layer of multiple machines send too many packets at high speed, the network will be quickly overloaded and productivity of the system will sharply fall causing delay and packet loss. Congestion control, aimed at combating such situations requires collaboration between the network and transport layers. Since overload occurs on routers, their discovery has been on the side of network layer of TCP/IP protocol stack. However the reason for congestion is the traffic transmitted by the transport layer. Therefore, the only effective way to control congestion is slower packet transmission by transport protocols and algorithms. Weighted random early detection (WRED) is a queuing discipline for a network scheduler suited for congestion avoidance. It has an advantage in comparison with other congestion control techniques, but at the same time requires very correct settings. This paper examines the algorithm of the selecting the correct setting for the WRED algorithm on the example of the widespread corporate networks.

Keywords: Networks · Congestion · Random early detection · WRED algorithm

1 Introduction

At the early stage of Internet usage the main advantage of packet data was the opportunity to create reliable networks capable of transmitting data flows over long distances, but now what comes to the fore is the ability of modern packet switched technologies to ensure the specified quality of service (QoS). In order to provide the necessary requirements for the different data streams two methods of QoS are used: congestion management and congestion avoidance. In [1], first method described as a method based on assigning quotas and priorities to the data streams, where in case of overload, the streams are limited by their quota and priority, for example, Weighted Fair Queuing (WFQ). Also in [1], the second method limits the size of the queue thereby indicating data source when it is necessary to reduce the data transmission rate, eg., Random Early Detection (RED). There is enough active research on methods of limiting the

© Springer International Publishing Switzerland 2015
R. Horne (Ed.): EGC 2015, CCIS 514, pp. 31–42, 2015.
DOI: 10.1007/978-3-319-25043-4_4

size of the queue. It is possible to list only a few, well-known modifications of RED algorithm: WRED, GRED (Gentle RED), DRED (Dynamic RED), SRED (Stabilized RED), ARED (Adaptive RED), RED-PD. The WRED algorithm is highly relevant and interesting to telecommunication scientists, the following only some of the pioneer-scientists working on the problem of preventing and combating congestion: Sally Floyd, Van Jacobson, Kevin Fall, Ratul Mahajan, Martin May, Jean Bolot, Vishal Misra, WeiBo Gong, Don Towsley, Thomas Ziegler, David Wetherall and others [2]. Despite of the great importance of the theme of congestion preventing, the problem of the setting parameters for the WRED algorithm remains. The exploration of the process of using the WRED algorithm is described in [3], where the WRED parameters also were examined for various traffic scenarios. Telecommunication companies always face the problem of congestion at the clients equipment and the WRED algorithm is one of the main techniques for preventing overloads. Hence this mechanism is implemented on almost all modern routers; while the remaining modifications have few practical implementation on network devices, at least in Kazakhtelecom company, where these experiments were conducted. Many network scientists and engineers agree with the statement that the WRED algorithm's influence on data stream QoS depends on the correct settings, but there are no intelligible instructions how in practice to choose values of these parameters. In this paper, the influence of parameters on the WRED algorithm execution is considered, and also instructions on choosing the optimal settings of the algorithm in the case of the geographically distributed network are given. The study was conducted on Cisco Systems hardware using the traffic generator software IxChariot.

2   WRED Features

The distinguishing feature of the WRED algorithm is that the decision on packet queuing is differently adapted, depending on the queue length. WRED uses the same parameters as RED, but it has the ability to perform RED on traffic classes individually [3]. From [2,4], the WRED mechanism uses the following parameters: w_q – the averaging weights; T_{MIN} – the lower threshold of average queue length; T_{MAX} – the upper threshold of average queue length; p_c – the maximum packet drop probability for the area between T_{MIN} and T_{MAX}. In the WRED set there are two thresholds T_{MIN} and T_{MAX}. While the average queue length is less than T_{MIN}, any incoming packet arrives to the buffer. In the region between T_{MIN} and T_{MAX} the risk of dropping the packet grows linearly from 0 to the value of p_c. The graph of the probability of packet dropping by WRED mechanism is shown in the Fig. 1.

After reaching the T_{MAX} threshold, all incoming packets are dropped. The average queue length depends on the previous average as well as the current length of the queue. Averaging the queue length is made according to the formula indicated below.

$$\overline{q}(k + 1) = (1 - w_q)\overline{q}(k) + w_q q(k) \tag{1}$$

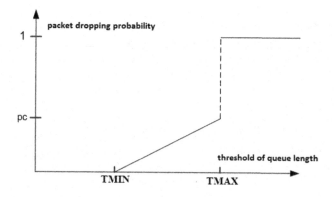

Fig. 1. Probability of packet dropping by WRED mechanism.

In the formula mentioned above, q (k + 1) is the average queue length at the $(k + 1)^{th}$ time, w_q is the averaging parameter, $\overline{q}$ and q is the average and current queue length at the kth time respectively [5]. For a small value of w_q the WRED process does not immediately start to drop packets on overload, but will continue to drop packets, even when there is no congestion (all fell below T_{MIN}). Correct averaging of queue length is a very important component of the control buffering process. Without averaging process buffering would be exposed to the strong influence of random fluctuations in the incoming packet stream, but it is also the cause of average queue length oscillation [6]. The dependence of the decision on packet dropping is determined by the averaged queue length, which may significantly differ from the value of the current queue length.

The main objective of the paper is an experimental study of the influence of the WRED algorithm parameters and to find the optimal parameters for a given level of overload. An experimental model was created where two remote offices were connected through the Internet Service Provider (ISP). The studies were conducted on Cisco Systems equipment: on the access layer of the central and branch offices networks Cataslist 2960 switches were used, Cisco ISR 2811 routers were involved as a boundary equipment to connect to the service provider routers. The distance between the two offices is about 3000 km, which is a frequent occurrence not only in Kazakhstan, but also in other countries. The experimental model is shown in the Fig. 2. Point-to-point connection between two offices in Almaty and Atyrau are organized with the help of GRE tunneling technology (without an IPSec protocol settings). The channel capacity connecting offices is 2 Mbit/s, due to limitations of the backbone network of ISP. In order to generate heterogeneous traffic, the IxChariot traffic generator software was used.

The real situation on the parts of the network was created by traffic generator; the narrow portion of the network in an experimental model is the channel between the remote offices routers with significant low bandwidth. The data transfer rate within the LAN is 100 Mbit/s, and the channel that connects a central office LAN and its branch has a bandwidth of 2 Mbit/s. Generated traffic

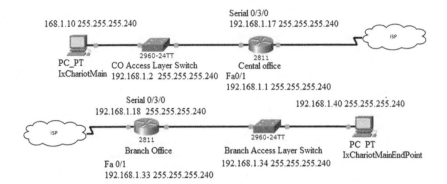

Fig. 2. An experimental model.

Fig. 3. The running configurations for the Central office router of the experimental model.

goes to the border router without loss and delay and, on the output of the router towards the network service provider interface, buffer overload occurs, which leads to great losses of packets and sensitive delay. Our study was conducted exactly in this area according to the dependence of congestion behavior on the WRED protocol parameters changing.

In the experimental streams of UDP (User Datagram Protocol) and TCP (Transmission Control Protocol) packets were transmitted through a test channel between two border routers. The WRED mechanism was configured on the routers with the default settings, and then by changing the values of these WRED parameters, the effect of these changes on the behavior of the overload. The idea for such approach for detecting ideal parameters is borrowed from [7,8]. The

Table 1. Some of the traffic generated by the IxChariot.

Pair	End point 1	End point 2	Protocol	Priority	Script/Flow name
IP telephony					
1	192.168.1.10	192.168.1.40	RTP	EF/5	G.726
2	192.168.1.10	192.168.1.40	RTP	EF/5	G.726
3	192.168.1.10	192.168.1.40	RTP	EF/5	G.711u
...	...	...	...	...	...
Internet					
13	192.168.1.10	192.168.1.40	TCP	AF21/2	DNS
14	192.168.1.10	192.168.1.40	TCP	AF21/2	HTTPS
15	192.168.1.10	192.168.1.40	TCP	AF21/2	SMTP
16	192.168.1.10	192.168.1.40	TCP	AF21/2	POP3
17	192.168.1.10	192.168.1.40	TCP	AF21/2	NNTP
...	...	...	...	...	...
Lotus notes					
25	192.168.1.10	192.168.1.40	TCP	AF11/1	Notes Attach
26	192.168.1.10	192.168.1.40	TCP	AF11/1	Notes Browser
27	192.168.1.10	192.168.1.40	TCP	AF11/1	Notes Create Note
28	192.168.1.10	192.168.1.40	TCP	AF11/1	Notes Indexed
...	...	...	...	...	...
Management					
35	192.168.1.10	192.168.1.40	TCP	AF31/3	Exchsend
36	192.168.1.10	192.168.1.40	TCP	AF31/3	Telnet
37	192.168.1.10	192.168.1.40	TCP	AF31/3	Citrix Server
...	...	...	...	...	...
SAP					
49	192.168.1.10	192.168.1.40	TCP	AF41/4	SAP R3
50	192.168.1.10	192.168.1.40	TCP	AF41/4	SAPlogin
51	192.168.1.10	192.168.1.40	TCP	AF41/4	SAPPauthp
...	...	...	...	...	...
SAP					
56	192.168.1.10	192.168.1.40	TCP	BE/0	FTPget
57	192.168.1.10	192.168.1.40	TCP	BE/0	FTPput
58	192.168.1.10	192.168.1.40	TCP	BE/0	eDonkeyPublicize
...	...	...	...	...	...
69	192.168.1.10	192.168.1.40	TCP	BE/0	eDonkeyDownload

results of the experiment were obtained at the endpoints of the traffic generator and from the statistical outputs of the router.

Figure 3 shows the running configurations for the Central office router of the experimental model. Further, based on [9], Table 1 shows some types of traffic generated by IxChariot.

3   Experiments

3.1   Study of the p_c Parameter Influence to the WRED Algorithm

In the 2nd paragraph was stated that p_c determines the maximum packet drop probability for the area between T_{MIN} and T_{MAX}. In the first experiment, the influence of the p_c parameter on the data flows through the WRED algorithm was considered. In the experiment, it was possible to smoothly change the value of p_c at the router interfaces. The routers p_c parameter is defined as the fraction $1/k$, where k is an integer in the range between 1 and 65535. The 6 flows were transmitted through the test channel, parameters of which are shown in Table 2.

The p_c value varied in the range between 0.001 and 1. Full capacity of the test channel was 2 Mbit/s. In the experiment, for each value of the p_c, three dimensions were done. Each experiment took about 1 min. For each measurement the dependence of the lost packets number for the different flows from the p_c parameter was obtained. Figure 4 shows the dependence of the loss percentage from the p_c parameter for different traffic priorities.

It can be seen that the values of $p_c < 0.25$ cause the same response of the system. The percentage of packet loss for the different p_c values are approximately same. The p_c parameter only affects the transition process that occurs when you overload the channel. Based on the results, we found that the percentage of packet loss is smallest at around $1/10$, which is the default p_c value on the Cisco routers. And so, for a given value of w_q reasonable value to use $p_c = 1/10$. The p_c parameter has very little effect on the percentage of packet loss in the case of channel overload. The p_c settings affects the duration of the initial transition process, but has no effect on the transmission characteristics of the packet flow during prolonged constant overloading.

The sharp increase in packet delivery delay occurs when the current queue WRED is growing, and the average length of the queue has not yet reached the

Table 2. The WRED parameters for the test flows.

IP precedence	w_q	T_{MIN}	T_{MAX}
0	1/512	20	40
1	1/512	22	40
2	1/512	24	40
3	1/512	26	40
4	1/512	28	40
5	1/512	31	40

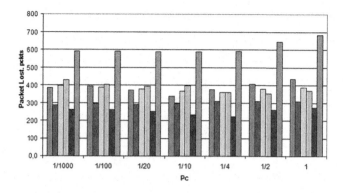

Fig. 4. The p_c parameter influence to the number of lost packets.

threshold TMAX. When the average queue length reaches the upper threshold, the current length of the queue begins to decline rapidly since all of packets arriving at the input are dropped. For different values of p_c transition time will be different. But of course the steady state of the system is the same for all values of p_c. The p_c parameter is important in the case of short-term overload, when the system does not have time to go to the stationary mode. We also found that the delay and jitter values do not depend on the p_c, the average delay at the time of the experiments was 164 ms, while jitter was 18.3 ms.

3.2   Study of the w_q Parameter Influence to the WRED Algorithm

In determining the probability of packet dropping mechanism WRED algorithm calculates not current, but the exponentially weighted average queue size. Current average queue size is determined based on the previous average and the current actual size. Using the mechanism of WRED average queue size is due to the desire to respond only to continuous network congestion and to ignore momentary bursts of traffic. In the second experiment, the influence of the w_q averaging weights coefficient was considered. The w_q parameter is responsible for the amplitude of the queue lengths oscillation, as well as the WRED algorithm reaction time to the overload fluctuations. The same flows as in the previous measurements were transmitted through the channel; the flows were labeled according to their priority value. In the experiment, it was possible to smoothly change the w_q parameter value at the router interface. The routers w_q parameter is defined as the fraction $1/2n$, where integer n - is an exponential weighting factor lies in the range between 1 and 16. The WRED algorithm settings for the transmitted flows were as follows: T_{MIN} is default values for each priority, $T_{MAX} = 40$, $p_c = 1/10$. Measurements were performed with the following w_q parameter values: $1/2, 1/4, 1/16, 1/512, 1/4096, 1/65536$. Measuring results of the lost packets number depending on the w_q parameter presented in the Table 3.

Table 3. The w_q parameter influence to the number of lost packets.

w_q/Priority	0	1	2	3	4	5
1/2	481	195	107	219	24	303
1/4	433	135	100	188	21	296
1/16	419	136	94	169	26	291
1/512	343	131	82	210	25	266
1/4096	431	138	94	244	32	448
1/65536	557	159	136	248	51	604

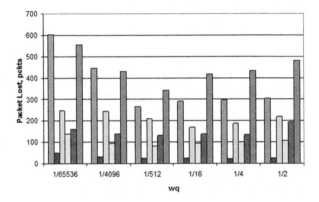

Fig. 5. The w_q parameter influence to the number of lost packets.

The exponential weighting factor is a key parameter that determines the relative contribution of the previous average and the current size of the queue in the new average queue size. Increasing the exponential weighting factor will lead to the domination of the previous average queue size of its current size in terms of the calculation of the new average queue size. Conversely, the decrease in the exponential weighting factor will result the increase in the importance of the current size of the queue in the calculation of its new average queue size.

Figure 5 show that for small values of the w_q parameters, the percentage of lost packets is maximal, which can be explained by the fact that for the large values of the exponential weighting the RED mechanism may stop responding to the network congestion, because in this case, the current size of the queue will have virtually no impact on the calculation of its average size. The packets are transmitted or dropped as if the RED mechanism is not used. In this case, the number of dropped packets by the Tail Drop mechanism significantly prevails over the number of dropped packets by the WRED algorithm. And vice versa, for large values of the w_q parameter we have a large percentage of lost packets, but in this case a larger number of packets lost were dropped by the WRED mechanism. In this situation, the WRED mechanism begins to be very sensitive to the temporary traffic bursts, resulting in unjustified packets drops.

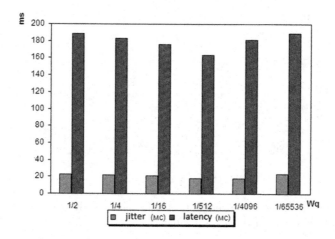

Fig. 6. The dependency of the average values of latency, jitter and MOS parameter from the w_q parameter.

Table 4. The WRED parameters for the test flows.

IP precedence	w_q	T_{MIN}	p_c
0	1/512	20	1/10
1	1/512	22	1/10
2	1/512	24	1/10
3	1/512	26	1/10
4	1/512	28	1/10
5	1/512	31	1/10

Minimal percentage of lost packets was found when w_q parameter is 1/512. Additionally, the influence of the w_q parameter to average values of packet transfer delay and jitter was found. Figure 6 show the relation of the average values of the latency and jitter and the Mean Opinion Score (MOS) parameter from the w_q parameter. MOS is a test that has been used for decades in telephony networks to obtain the human user's view of the quality of the network.Improving of the average subjective MOS scores is the result of the reducing the delays for voice traffic. The best quality of the telephone conversation was recorded at the value $w_q = 1/16$, at the same mark were the minimal values of the delay and jitter of voice traffic (Table 4).

3.3 Study of the T_{MIN} and T_{MAX} Thresholds Influence to the WRED Algorithm

In the third experiment, the effect of the T_{MIN} and the T_{MAX} thresholds for the WRED algorithm were investigated. The WRED algorithm thresholds affect

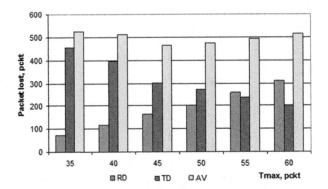

Fig. 7. The dependency of the average packet lost, caused by the Random Drop and Tail Drop mechanism, from the T_{MAX} value.

the minimum and maximum packets delay time in the case of overload. During the third experiment, the amount of traffic generated and intensity remained constant. The lower thresholds of the WRED algorithm for different priorities had not changed either. The value of the upper threshold T_{MAX} has changed in the range between 35 and 60 packets with increments of the 5 packets. It makes no sense to put a large threshold of the T_{MAX}, since the duration of the overload buffer overflow occurs, allotted on the outgoing interface of the router under the batch queue. For the p_c parameter value $= 1/10$ correlation between the values of the average delay and packet loss and the value for T_{MAX} for voice traffic with priority equal 5 was received, the correlation of the jitter when transmitting voice packet was measured.

Correlation in Fig. 7 show the packet loss in the transmission of the voice traffic for the different values of the threshold T_{MAX} value. Figure 7 shows that when the value of the maximum T_{MAX} threshold is changed, in addition to changing the value of the lost packets, the reason for the router of packet drop also seems to change. If the value is close to the minimum threshold of discarding the time to reach the maximum queue threshold is significantly reduced, thus the work of the Tail Drop mechanism begins much earlier. This is the reason a large number of the dropped packets by the Tail Drop mechanism. Furthermore, an increase in T_{MAX}, increases the percentage of the dropped packets mechanism by the Random Drop, due to the longer time required to reach the stage of T_{MAX}. Hence, the Random Drop mechanism begins to dominate, respectively, packet loss caused by the Tail Drop mechanism is reduced [10]. As can be seen from the graph, the average value of the packet lost at very small and very large values of the T_{MAX} is maximal. The optimal value of the threshold T_{MAX} value is 45.

Correlation in Fig. 8 show the behavior of the packets transmission delay from the different values of the T_{MAX} threshold. At high values for T_{MAX} there is maximum delay that is caused by an increase in latency of sending a packet to

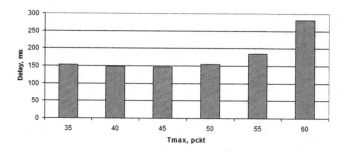

Fig. 8. The dependency between the transmission delay of voice traffic and the T_{MAX} value.

the buffer interface. It was also measured the MOS coefficient. The maximum value of the MOS is 3,23, as observed when T_{MAX} equals to 45.

4   Conclusions

After conducting the experiments on the WRED algorithm parameters, it can be seen that the recommended settings of equipment vendor may not always be absolutely correct and suitable for the configuration of specific networks. In our case, through extensive experimentation, we found that the default settings in Cisco routers are not suitable for connecting relatively distant sites. For such situations the best WRED algorithm parameters which prevent congestion in the network on the best way were found as follows: $p_c = 1/10$, $w_q = 1/16$ and $T_{MAX} = 45$, which are slightly different from the Cisco Systems offering default settings. Moreover by creating simple script the process of finding and installing the optimal settings can be automated. Such approach of defining ideal WRED parameters can be useful during the construction the large distributed network especially on huge geographical area where communication links between devices are absolutely different on their supported QoS characteristics.

The investigation and the results obtained certainly have great practical significance. Because the algorithm of preventing congestion is used by the majority of service providers, and we found the parameters are suitable for any of them. When using the obtained settings WRED algorithm can significantly change the behavior of congestion at the router level. Correctly tuned mechanism of congestion prevention can completely eliminate congestion in networks with constant traffic intensity.

References

1. Tanenbaum, A.S., Wetherall, D.J.: Computer Networks, 5th edn. Pearson, Saddle River (2011)
2. Floyd, S., Jacobson, V.: Random early detection gateway for congestion avoidance. IEEE/ACM Trans. Netw. **1**, 397–413 (2010)

3. Wurtzler, M.: Analysis and Simulation of Weighted Random Early Detection (WRED) Queues. Northwestern University, BSEE, Evanston (2002)
4. Cisco IOS Quality of Service Solutions Configuration Guide. Congestion Avoidance Overview. Cisco, Accessed 18 June 2014
5. Cisco IOS Release 12.0(26)S. Class-Based Weighted Fair Queueing and Weighted Random Early Detection. Cisco, Accessed 18 June 2014
6. Froom, R., Flannagan, M., Turek, K.: Quality of Service in Campus Networks. Cisco Press, Indianapolis (2012)
7. Goncharov, A., Ilyin, A., Semenov, Y.: Possibilities of obtaining guaranteed quality of service. Information Processes (2006)
8. Goncharov, A., Ilyin, A., Semenov, A.: Study opportunities for quality of service in the transmission of multimedia through the congested channels. Information Processes (2006)
9. Alvarez, S.: QoS for IP Networks. Cisco Press, Indianapolis (2010)
10. Szigeti, T., Hattingh, C.: End-to-End QoS Network Design. Cisco Press, Indianapolis (2004)

Mobility Types for Cloud Computing

Bogdan Aman$^{(\boxtimes)}$ and Gabriel Ciobanu

Institute of Computer Science, Romanian Academy,
Blvd. Carol I No. 08, 700505 Iaşi, Romania
baman@iit.tuiasi.ro, gabriel@info.uaic.ro

Abstract. We propose a mobility type system for description and verification of distributed systems in which processes are asked to move between locations where important local interactions are required. We use a simple version of distributed π-calculus to define mobility types. The novelty of this approach is that we point out sequences of migrations as global types, and investigate scenarios in which processes are required to follow such a sequence of migrations along several locations. The typing system ensures certain properties including type soundness.

1 Introduction

Cloud computing is a paradigm combining different aspects of computing, by providing both flexibility and mobility of information. In recent years the cloud computing and mobile computing have started to converge, as the interaction capabilities of mobile devices can be fused with processing in the cloud [9]. Mobility plays an important role in developing a new generation of mobile applications. Mobility provides the ability of applications to move between locations and devices during their execution. This means that a running application migrates from one location/device to another depending on the proximity of the user.

A mobile application is closely related to process migration in distributed systems modelled by process calculi such as distributed π-calculus ($D\pi$) [10] and TIMO (Timed Mobility) [7]. The migration of processes represents the capability of a running process to be relocated from a location to another one in order to access data locally. In order to have a seamless migration, cloudlets are used to eliminate the inherent latency of migration in wide-area networks [15]. A cloudlet is a trusted resource rich computing infrastructure with high-speed Internet connectivity to the cloud. It is available for use by nearby mobile devices and offers similar services as the cloud, but more quickly. A mobile client can use any cloudlet from its proximity in order to deploy all of its significant computation in that cloudlet.

Significant efforts have been devoted to build secure (mobile) cloud computing environments [12]. In this paper we propose a formalism to describe and reason over migrating processes and their behaviour. The basic idea is to introduce mobility types that allow typing by structured sequences of types, abstractly representing an uninterrupted sequence of migrations for processes. Typing locations with mobility types (while disregarding the local communication) is sufficient to

© Springer International Publishing Switzerland 2015
R. Horne (Ed.): EGC 2015, CCIS 514, pp. 43–53, 2015.
DOI: 10.1007/978-3-319-25043-4_5

detect subtle errors in the implementation of mobile applications and protocols. We do not insist on typing the local communication inside locations as it has been proposed by session types [16] and contracts [13]. Session types are used to reason over communicating processes and their behaviour by abstractly representing the trace of the usage of the channels as a structured sequences of types. A detailed discussion and analysis of several versions of the π-calculi with session types is given in [17]. On the other hand, contracts are behavioural descriptions of Web services [3] that record the overall behaviour of a process, in contrast with session types that project this behaviour onto the private channels that a process uses.

The rest of this paper is organised as follows: Sect. 2 presents the syntax and semantics of a calculus able to naturally describe migration. Section 3 provides the mobility types. Section 4 concludes the paper.

2   Describing Mobile Applications for Cloudlets

In order to handle distributed interaction patterns described by cloud algorithms, we propose a novel mobility calculus in which the migration of processes is performed only by agreement and is done through access ports. In the current paper we use migrating processes that are asked to move to given locations where necessary (local) communications are required. As a case study we consider mobile applications moving between cloudlets and user devices.

2.1   Syntax

The syntax for processes is based on distributed π-calculus [10] and user-defined processes [11]. The syntax is given in Table 1, where we assume:

- a set Loc of locations, a set $Port$ of access ports, and a set Id of process identifiers (each $id \in Id$ has its arity m_{id});
- for each $id \in Id$ there is a unique process definition $id(u_1, \ldots, u_{m_{id}}) \stackrel{def}{=} P_{id}$, where the distinct variables u_i are parameters;
- $a \in Port$ is a communication port; l is a location or a location variable (can be assigned dynamically through communication); t is a tag;
- v is a tuple of expressions built from values, variables and allowed operations.

The prefix $go\ l(a).P$ initiates a migration by accessing a port a at location l; this happens only if a process of the form $(a).Q$ exists at location l. The name a is used as a communication port for internal communication between the continuing processes P and Q. Local communications inside a location are performed using the next two pairs of primitives: the sending and receiving, and the selection and branching (the latter offers a multitude of branches from which the former chooses one). The conditional branching, parallel composition and inaction are standard constructions. The recursion realizes the recursive behaviour. The notions of bound and free identifiers, alpha-equivalence and substitution are standard.

Table 1. Syntax

Processes	P, Q $::=$	$go\ l(a).P$	(migration)
	$\mid$	$(a).P$	(offering port)
	$\mid$	$a!\langle v \rangle.P$	(sending)
	$\mid$	$a?(u).P$	(receiving)
	$\mid$	$a \triangleleft t.P$	(tag selection)
	$\mid$	$a \triangleright \{t_i : P_i\}_{i \in I}$	(tag branching)
	$\mid$	if e then P else Q	(conditional branching)
	$\mid$	$P \mid Q$	(parallel composition)
	$\mid$	0	(inaction)
	$\mid$	$\mu X.P$	(recursion)
	$\mid$	X	(variable)
Located processes	L $::=$	$l[[P]]$	
Networks	N $::=$	L	(located processes)
	$\mid$	$L \mid N$	(parallel composition)

2.2   Operational Semantics

Structural congruence $\equiv$ is the smallest congruence relation on networks that includes the equations in Table 2.

Table 2. Structural congruence

(NNULL)	$N \mid l[[0]] \equiv N$
(NCOMM)	$N \mid N' \equiv N' \mid N$
(NASSOC)	$(N \mid N') \mid N'' \equiv N \mid (N' \mid N'')$
(NSPLIT)	$l[[P \mid Q]] \equiv l[[P]] \mid l[[Q]]$

The operational semantics is given by a reduction relation denoted $M \to N$, which is the smallest relation generated by the rules in Table 3, where $e \downarrow v$ says that expression e is evaluated to values v.

Table 3. Operational semantics

$k[[go\ l(a).P \mid Q]] \mid l[[(a).R]] \to k[[Q]] \mid l[[P \mid R]]$	(MIGRATE)
$l[[a!\langle v \rangle.P \mid a?(u).Q]] \to l[[P \mid Q\{v/u\}]]$	(COMM)
$l[[a \triangleleft t_j.P \mid a \triangleright \{t_i.P_i\}_{i \in I}]] \to l[[P \mid P_j]] \ (j \in J)$	(BRANCH)
$l[[R \mid \text{if } e \text{ then } P \text{ else } Q]] \to l[[R \mid P]] \ (e \downarrow true)$	(IFT)
$l[[R \mid \text{if } e \text{ then } P \text{ else } Q]] \to l]]R \mid Q]] \ (e \downarrow false)$	(IFF)
$l[[\mu X.P \mid Q]] \to l[[P\{\mu X.P/X\} \mid Q]]$	(CALL)
$N \to N' \Rightarrow N \mid N_1 \to N' \mid N_1$	(PAR)
$N \equiv N_1 \text{ and } N_1 \to N_1' \text{ and } N_1' \equiv N' \Rightarrow N \to N'$	(STRUCT)

Rule (MIGRATE) describes migration of processes between locations by using a port available at the destination location where the parties can communicate in order to establish necessary local interactions (using this port). (COMM) is the standard communication rule derived from π-calculus, where the received value v replaces the existing free occurrences of u in Q. E.g., consider a process that needs the $sqrt$ of v and knows that there is a process able to compute it. In this case it sends the value v on channel a and continues it execution as P, while the process receiving the value makes the calculations by executing $Q\{v/u\}$. Rule (BRANCH) selects the corresponding branch. The process $a \triangleright \{t_i.P_i\}_{i \in I}$ offers a multitude of branches from which the process $a \triangleleft t_j.P$ chooses one (depending on its previous computation or on its context). The other rules are rather standard.

2.3   Example

We consider a mobile device trying to discover and connect to a cloudlet infrastructure (see Fig. 1). If the negotiation was successful, it sends an application to the cloudlet which starts executing depending on the received application. Once the computation is finished, the mobile device receives some data and departs from the cloudlet. For instance, the cloudlet could be a server that receives some image from a mobile device, performs some face recognition algorithms, and then returns the output. According to [15], it is easy for a mobile device to find a cloudlet to interact with even when it is far from home.

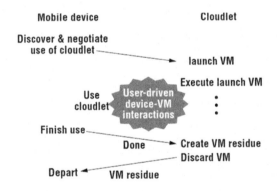

Fig. 1. Interaction between a mobile device and a cloudlet (adapted from [15])

In what follows, we use a very simple example to illustrate the features of our approach. We abstract from any other processes present in the mobile device or the cloudlet, from the local communications and from what happens after the cloudlet returns the recognition output, regardless of the fact that the recognition is successful or not. Such a system can be formalised as the network:

$$MobDev[[SendImage]] \mid Cloudlet[[FaceApp]]$$

We now describe the behaviour of the *SendImage* application as a process:
$SendImage = go\ Cloudlet(a) \ldots$

$\qquad a \rhd \{ok : 0, quit : 0\}$
$\qquad | \ go\ Cloudlet(b) \ | \ (c)$

The mobile device send to a cloudlet an application that has an image to be recognised (the process starting with *go*). After some local communications which we omitted (and thus denoted by ...), depending on the successfulness of the recognition, the mobile process (now placed in the cloudlet) selects what it does next. The device either sends to the cloudlet a new process on port b with some informations, or waits for process on port c denoting a failed recognition attempt. The cloudlet can be described as the process:
$FaceApp = (a) \ldots$

$\qquad if(recognized)$
$\qquad\qquad then\ a \lhd ok : ((b).0)$
$\qquad\qquad else\ a \lhd quit : (go\ MobDev(c).0)$

After receiving an image to be recognised, the cloudlet performs some local communications which we omitted (and thus denoted by ...). Depending on the successfulness of the recognition, the cloudlet device waits for a process on port b with some new request (label ok), or sends a process on port c denoting a failed recognition attempt (label $quit$).

3   Mobility Types

A basic observation underlying mobility types is that a mobile application often exhibits sequences of migrations involving branching and recursion. We abstract such a sequence of migrations as a type in order to validate the migration behaviours. The communication inside locations can be typed using session types [16] and contracts [13]; we avoid typing local communications in this paper, focusing on mobility typing.

3.1   Global Types

The global types (ranged over by $G, G', \ldots$) describe the global behaviour of the system, being presented in Table 4. Type $l \to l' : a.G'$ says that from location l a process migrates to location l' through the access port a, where the

Table 4. Syntax of global types

Global G $::=$	$l \to l' : a.G'$	(processes)
|	$l : a\{t_i : G_i\}_{i \in I}$	(branching)
|	G, G'	(parallel)
|	$\mu t.G$	(recursive)
|	t	(variable)
|	end	(end)

process behaves accordingly to the mobility type described by G'. We assume that in each prefix $l \to l'$ from l to l' we have $l \neq l'$, i.e. we prohibit reflexive interaction. Type $l : a\{t_i : G_i\}_{i \in I}$ says that at location l one process sends one of the tags t_i, using port a, to another process. If t_j is sent, migration described by type G_j takes place. Type G, G' represents concurrent run of migrations specified by G and G'. Type $\mu t.G$ is a recursive type for migration structures, where type variable t is guarded in the standard way (they only appear under some prefix). Even if t is overloaded, it will result from the context what it represents. Type end represents the termination of a process. We identify both G, end and end, G with G.

Example 1. A global type of the translation protocol in Subsect. 2.3:
$$G = MobDev \to Cloudlet : a.$$
$$Cloudlet : a\{ok : (MobDev \to Cloudlet : b),$$
$$quit : (Cloudlet \to MobDev : c)\}$$
Consider that the process *FaceApp* does not notify the *MobDev* about the failure of recognition, denoted by the missing of the action *go MobDev(c)*:
$$FaceApp = (a) \dots if(recognized)$$
$$then \ a \lhd ok : ((b).0)$$
$$else \ a \lhd quit : (\overline{go \ MobDev(c)}.0)$$
In this case the *FaceApp* process does not behave as intended, namely as described by the global type G.

3.2 Local Types

Local types (ranged over by $T, T', \dots$) are presented in Table 5; they describe the local behaviour of processes, acting as a link between global types and processes. Type $a!.T$ represents the behaviour of sending a process on port (a) and then behaving as described by type T. Similarly $a?.T$ is for receiving, and continuing as described by local type T. Type $a\&\{t_i : Ti\}_{i \in I}$ describes a branching: it waits with $|I|$ options at a, and behaves as type T_i if i-th tag is selected; type $a \oplus \{t_i : T_i\}_{i \in I}$ represents the behaviour which selects one of the tags, e.g. t_i at a

Table 5. Syntax of local types

$Local\ T$	$::=$	$a!.T$	(send)
	$\mid$	$a?.T$	(receive)
	$\mid$	$a \oplus \{t_i : T_i\}_{i \in I}$	(selection)
	$\mid$	$a\&\{t_i : T_i\}_{i \in I}$	(branching)
	$\mid$	T, T'	(parallel)
	$\mid$	$\mu t.T$	(recursive)
	$\mid$	t	(variable)
	$\mid$	end	(end)

and then behaves as T_i. The rest is the same as for the global types, demanding type variables occur guarded by a prefix. We often omit end by identifying both T, end and end, T with T.

Example 2. The local types of the translate protocol in Subsect. 2.3:

$$T_{MobDev} = a!, b!, c?$$
$$T_{Cloudlet} = a?.(a \oplus \{ok : b?, quit : c!\}, a\&\{ok : end, quit : end\})$$

We now illustrate the connection between global and local types by defining the projection operation $G \uparrow l$ which, for a location l appearing in a global type G, provides the local type it has to conform to. The projection is inductively given as:

- $l_1 \to l_2 : a.G \uparrow l = \begin{cases} a!.G \uparrow l & \text{if } l = l_1 \\ a?.G \uparrow l. & \text{if } l = l_2 \end{cases};$

- $l_1 : a\{t_i : G_i\}_{i \in I} \uparrow l = \begin{cases} a \oplus \{t_i : G_i \uparrow l\}, a\&\{t_i : G_i \uparrow l\} & \text{if } l = l_1 \\ end & \text{otherwise} \end{cases};$

- $G, G' \uparrow l = G \uparrow l, G' \uparrow l;$
- $t \uparrow l = t;$
- end $\uparrow l = $ end.

Example 3. For the example of Subsect. 2.3, starting from the global type G of Example 1, we obtain the local types of Example 2, namely

$$G \uparrow MobDev = T_{MobDev} \text{ and } G \uparrow Cloudlet = T_{Cloudlet}.$$

3.3   Typing System

Here we introduce the typing system. Considering $\Gamma, \Gamma', \ldots :: = \emptyset \mid \Gamma, G \mid \Gamma,$ $X : \Delta$ record the global type and the assignments to variables. $\Delta, \Delta' \ldots = \emptyset \mid \Delta, l : T$ records the local types at each location involved in the typed network. The type assignment system for processes is given in Table 6. We use the judgement $\Gamma \vdash N \rhd \Delta$ which says that "under the environment Γ, network N has typing Δ".

(Bool) states that under any environment *true* and *false* are boolean values. Rule (End) associates to each empty location $l[[0]]$ present in the network with the termination type end. (Migration) is the rule for initiating a migration. The prefix $a!$, for migration, is added to the local type of location l, while what was at location l (the type of P), is moved to the local type of location l'. On the hand, the rule (Accept Migration) is for accepting an initiated migration by agreeing on the communication port. The relevant type prefix $a?$, for acceptance, is composed in the conclusion's local type of location l. Rules (Send) and (Receive) are used for communication, and so they do not affect the mobility part.

(Select) and (Branch) are the rules for selection and branching; in the rules for migration the information about local types is updated depending on the used tags. To type check a branching process prefixed by a, (Branch) checks each of the possible continuations P_i even if only one of the P_i will be executed.

Table 6. Typing system

$\Gamma \vdash true, false : bool$	(Bool)
$\Gamma \vdash l[[0]] \triangleright l : \mathsf{end}$	(End)
$\dfrac{\Gamma \vdash l[[P]] \triangleright l : T}{\Gamma \vdash l[[go\ l'(a).P]] \triangleright l : a!, l' : T}$	(Migration)
$\dfrac{\Gamma \vdash l[[P]] \triangleright l : T}{\Gamma \vdash l[[(a).P]] \triangleright l : a?.T}$	(Accept Migration)
$\dfrac{\Gamma \vdash l[[P]] \triangleright \Delta}{\Gamma \vdash l[[a!\langle v \rangle.P]] \triangleright \Delta}$	(Send)
$\dfrac{\Gamma \vdash l[[P]] \triangleright \Delta}{\Gamma \vdash l[[a?(u).P]] \triangleright \Delta}$	(Receive)
$\dfrac{\Gamma \vdash l[[P]] \triangleright l : T}{\Gamma \vdash l[[a \triangleleft t.P]] \triangleright l : a \oplus \{t.T\}}$	(Select)
$\dfrac{\Gamma \vdash l[[P_i]] \triangleright l : T_i; \qquad \forall i \in I}{\Gamma \vdash l[[a \triangleright \{t_i : P_i\}_{i \in I}]] \triangleright l : a\&\{t_i : T_i\}_{i \in I}}$	(Branch)
$\dfrac{\Gamma \vdash e : bool; \qquad \Gamma \vdash l[[P]] \triangleright \Delta; \qquad \Gamma \vdash l[[Q]] \triangleright \Delta}{\Gamma \vdash l[[\ \text{if } e \text{ then } P \text{ else } Q]] \triangleright \Delta}$	(If)
$\dfrac{\Gamma \vdash N \triangleright \Delta; \qquad \Gamma \vdash N' \triangleright \Delta'; \qquad \Delta \bowtie \Delta'}{\Gamma \vdash N \mid N' \triangleright \Delta \uplus \Delta'}$	(Par)
$\dfrac{\Gamma, X : \Delta \vdash l[[P]] \triangleright \Delta}{\Gamma \vdash l[[\mu X.P]] \triangleright \Delta}$	(Rec)

If rule (Branch) introduces for location l an external choice type $a\&\{t_i : T_i\}_{i \in I}$, rule (Select) introduces the dual, internal choice type $a \oplus \{t.T\}$.

Rule (If) for the conditional process uses $bool$ to the type the condition and Δ for the two branches since only one of P or Q will be executed. (Par) uses $\bowtie$ to ensure well-formedness of the typing, taking a disjoint union of Δ used to type check network N and Δ' used to type check network N'. In typing a recursive process $\mu X.P$ at a location l, rule (Rec) assures that the type of P is the same as the type associated to X in the environment

Example 4. Consider the network of Subsect. 2.3. Its sub-networks, namely $MobDev[[SendText]]$ and $Cloudlet[[TransApp]]$, are typed as follows:
$$G \vdash MobDev[[SendImage]] \triangleright MobDev : a!, b!, c?$$
$$, Cloudlet : a\&\{ok : end, quit : end\}$$
$$G \vdash Cloudlet[[FaceApp]] \triangleright Cloudlet : a?.a \oplus \{ok : b?, quit : c!\}$$
The network is well-formed with respect to the global type G of Example 1. Applying the (Par) rule, for each location we obtain the local types of Example 2.

As processes interact, the types need to follow this evolution. This dynamics is formalised by a type reduction relation $\Rightarrow$ on environments Δ:
$$l : a!, T_1, l' : a?.T_2 \Rightarrow l : T_1, l' : T_2$$
$$l : a \oplus \{t_j.T'\}, a\&\{t_i.T_i\}_{i \in I} \Rightarrow T' \mid T_j \ (j \in J)$$

Now we present the main theoretical result of the paper.

Theorem 1. *(subject congruence and reduction).*

1. $\Gamma \vdash N \rhd \Delta$ and $N \equiv N'$ imply $\Gamma \vdash N' \rhd \Delta$.
2. $\Gamma \vdash N \rhd \Delta$ and $N \rightarrow N'$ imply $\Gamma \vdash N' \rhd \Delta'$, where $\Delta = \Delta'$ or $\Delta \Rightarrow \Delta'$.

Proof.   1. By induction on $\equiv$. We only only one case; the other cases are similar.

- $N \mid l[[0]] \equiv N$. First we assume $\Gamma \vdash N \rhd \Delta$. From $\Gamma \vdash l[[0]] \rhd l : end$ by applying (Par) to these two judgements, and ignoring the end type, we obtain $\Gamma \vdash N \mid l[[0]] \rhd \Delta$.

  For the converse direction assume $\Gamma \vdash N \mid l[[0]] \rhd \Delta$. To build a derivation for the conclusion we obtain: $\Gamma \vdash N \rhd \Delta_1$, $\Gamma \vdash l[[0]] \rhd \Delta_2$, where $\Delta = \Delta_1 \uplus \Delta_2$. According to rule (End), $\Gamma \vdash l[[0]] \rhd end$ meaning that $\Delta_2 = end$. Using that $\Delta = \Delta_1 \uplus \Delta_2$ and $\Delta_2 = end$ it results that $\Delta_1 = \Delta$ and thus $\Gamma \vdash N \rhd \Delta$.

2. The proof is by induction on the derivation $N \rightarrow N'$, with a case analysis on the final rule (using the previous item for the structural equivalence). We consider one case; the other cases are similar.

- $k[[go\ l(a).P \mid Q]] \mid l[[(a).R]] \rightarrow k[[Q]] \mid l[[P \mid R]]$ (MIGRATE)

  By hypothesis $\Gamma \vdash k[[go\ l(a).P \mid Q]] \mid l[[(a).R]] \rightarrow k[[Q]] \rhd \Delta$. Since this is a conclusion of two (Par) rules it has to be the case that:

  - $\Gamma \vdash k[[go\ l(a).P]] \rhd \Delta_1$

    This is obtained using (Migration) rule so $\Delta_1 = k : a!, l : T_P$ where T_P is the type of process P.
  - $\Gamma \vdash k[[Q]] \rhd \Delta_2$, where $\Delta_2 = k : T_Q$
  - $\Gamma \vdash l[[(a).R]] \rhd \Delta_3$

    This is obtained using (Accept Migration) rule so $\Delta_3 = \Delta_{33}, l : a?.T_R$ where T_R is the type of process R.
  - $\Delta = \Delta_1 \uplus \Delta_2 \uplus \Delta_3$ and $\Delta_1 \bowtie \Delta_2 \bowtie \Delta_3$

  After applying the (Migrate) rule, we obtain the term $k[[Q]] \mid l[[P \mid R]]$ such that $\Gamma \vdash k[[Q]] \mid l[[P \mid R]] \rhd \Delta'$ where, by a similar reasoning as above:

- $\Gamma \vdash l[[P]] \rhd \Delta_1'$, where $\Delta_1' = l : T_P$
- $\Gamma \vdash k[[Q]] \rhd \Delta_2'$, where $\Delta_2' = k : T_Q$
- $\Gamma \vdash l[[R]] \rhd \Delta_3'$, where $\Delta_3' = l : T_R$
- $\Delta' = \Delta_1' \uplus \Delta_2' \uplus \Delta_3'$ and $\Delta_1' \bowtie \Delta_2' \bowtie \Delta_3'$.

It can be noticed that $\Delta \Rightarrow \Delta'$ by applying the type reduction on environments:

$$k : a!, l : a?.T_P \Rightarrow k : end, l : T_P$$

and thus the proof for this case is completed.

4   Conclusion and Related Work

Trying to define a mobility version of session types, we emphasise on migration capabilities, in contrast with the typing system for distributed π-calculus [10] which uses types of the form $T@p$ and dependent type techniques, or that of mobile ambients [2] that guarantees the soundness of message exchanges, while leaving great flexibility in mobility. A version of session types in which executing processes are sent along channels is presented in [14], but the types are used for communication sessions and not for mobility as we do.

The simple mobility typing proposed here is related to TiMo [7] which is essentially a simpler version of timed distributed π-calculus [8]. TiMo can be seen as a prototyping language for multi-agent systems able to exploit in a unified framework features as relative time given by timers, timed migration and communication, explicit locations and local clocks in distributed systems [5]. Inspired by TiMo, a flexible software platform was introduced in [6] to support the specification of mobile agents allowing discovery of resources in a distributed environment [4]. A detailed view on mobility in both process calculi and natural computing is provided in [1].

Acknowledgements. Many thanks to the reviewers and to Ross Horne for their helpful comments. This paper is inspired by the COST Action IC1201. The work was supported by a grant of the Romanian National Authority for Scientific Research, project number PN-II-ID-PCE-2011-3-0919.

References

1. Aman, B., Ciobanu, G.: Mobility in Process Calculi and Natural Computing. Natural Computing Series. Springer, Heidelberg (2011)
2. Cardelli, L., Gordon, A.: Types for mobile ambients. In: Proceedings of POPL 1999, pp. 79–92. ACM Press (1999)
3. Castagna, G., Gesbert, N., Padovani, L.: A theory of contracts for web services. ACM Trans. Program. Lang. Syst. **31**(5), 51 (2009). article no.19
4. Ciobanu, G.: Finding network resources by using mobile agents. In: Essaaidi, M., Malgeri, M., Badica, C. (eds.) Intelligent Distributed Computing IV. SCI, vol. 315, pp. 305–313. Springer, Heidelberg (2010)
5. Ciobanu, G., Juravle, C.: A software platform for timed mobility and timed interaction. In: Lee, D., Lopes, A., Poetzsch-Heffter, A. (eds.) FMOODS 2009. LNCS, vol. 5522, pp. 106–121. Springer, Heidelberg (2009)
6. Ciobanu, G., Juravle, C.: Flexible software architecture and language for mobile agents. Concurrency Comput.: Pract. Exp. **24**, 559–571 (2012)
7. Ciobanu, G., Koutny, M.: Modelling and verification of timed interaction and migration. In: Fiadeiro, J.L., Inverardi, P. (eds.) FASE 2008. LNCS, vol. 4961, pp. 215–229. Springer, Heidelberg (2008)
8. Ciobanu, G., Prisacariu, C.: Timers for distributed systems. Electron. Notes Theoret. Comput. Sci. **164**(3), 81–99 (2006)
9. Fernando, N., Loke, S.W., Rahayu, W.: Mobile cloud computing: a survey. Future Gener. Comput. Syst. **29**(1), 84–106 (2013)

10. Hennessy, M.: A Distributed π-calculus. Cambridge University Press, Cambridge (2007)
11. Honda, K., Yoshida, N., Carbone, M.: Multiparty asynchronous session types. In: POPL 2008, pp. 273–284 (2008)
12. Khan, A.N., Kiah, M.L.M., Khan, S.U., Madani, S.A.: Towards secure mobile cloud computing: a survey. Future Gener. Comput. Syst. **29**, 1278–1299 (2013)
13. Meredith, G., Bjorg, S.: Contracts and types. Commun. ACM **46**(10), 41–47 (2003)
14. Mostrous, D., Yoshida, N.: Two session typing systems for higher-order mobile processes. In: Della Rocca, S.R. (ed.) TLCA 2007. LNCS, vol. 4583, pp. 321–335. Springer, Heidelberg (2007)
15. Satyanarayanan, M., Bahl, P., Caceres, R., Davies, N.: The case for VM-based cloudlets in mobile computing. IEEE Pervasive Comput. **8**(4), 14–23 (2009)
16. Takeuchi, K., Honda, K., Kubo, M.: An interaction-based language and its typing system. In: Halatsis, C., Philokyprou, G., Maritsas, D., Theodoridis, S. (eds.) PARLE 1994. LNCS, vol. 817. Springer, Heidelberg (1994)
17. Yoshida, N., Vasconcelos, V.T.: Language primitives and type discipline for structured communication-based programming revisited: two systems for higher-order session communication. Electron. Notes Theoret. Comput. Sci. **171**(4), 73–93 (2007)

Reversible Express Bus Lanes
Simulation Software

Timur Bakibayev[1]([✉]), Gulnara Bekmagambetova[2], and Asem Turarbek[3]

[1] ADA University, Baku, Azerbaijan
`timurbakibayev@gmail.com`
[2] Research Institute of Transport and Communication, Almaty, Kazakhstan
`gulnarabek@yahoo.com`
[3] Al-Farabi Kazakh National University, Almaty, Kazakhstan
`turarbek_asem@mail.ru`

Abstract. Exempting buses from other traffic seems to be an obviously good idea. On the other hand, it is not always possible to dedicate necessary space in the city for an extra lane. Therefore, our goal was to optimize the existing roads for giving priority to buses. Again, it would be nice to dedicate the rightmost lane to buses, but the other drivers would feel strong discomfort when turning right or parking. Moreover, this approach requires two lanes, one lane in each direction. So we tried to examine whether it makes sense to take the lane in the median area of the road, make it reversible and give it to buses.

In our work we simulated such a reversible bus lane. We simulate buses that have to change to the leftmost lane and then change back to the rightmost lane for a bus stop. This way we have found out the minimum distance between bus stops such that buses would be able to use it.

Keywords: Traffic simulation · Bus lanes · Reversible lanes

1 Introduction

Our aim was to simulate the traffic with a reversible bus lane in the median area of the road between the two opposite directions on a straight line of several lanes apart from the other streets.

In [1, 2] A. Valencia and R. Fernandez's presented a model for public transport corridors (CORBUS, CORridor for BUSes), which represents the progression of vehicles in consideration of all sources of potential delays at links, intersections, and stops. And while others (e.g. see [3, 4]) study the bus lanes with the bus stops next to the lanes, we tried to reserve a lane for buses without reconstructing the roads (e.g., building bus stops in the center of the roads). We decided to check whether it makes sense to dedicate a corridor for buses in the middle of the road keeping bus stops at the sidewalks.

© Springer International Publishing Switzerland 2015
R. Horne (Ed.): EGC 2015, CCIS 514, pp. 54–63, 2015.
DOI: 10.1007/978-3-319-25043-4_6

A microsimulation of the bus stops has been done by R. Fernandez in [5], where he showed the optimal distances to stop lines, distances between two buses, the optimal width of the bus stop, so that the bus stop could serve buses in parallel.

In this paper we show the minimum distances between bus stops in case of dedicating a reversible bus corridor in the median area of the road. For this reason we have implemented a software for a microsimulation of buses on such model taking into account the traffic density and the number of lanes. The idea is that if the bus stops are at the sidewalks, the bus has to go through the traffic to the leftmost lane (in the case of the right-hand traffic) and then return to the rightmost lane in order to stop. And this is the key point of our simulation - throughout the simulation the buses try to change to the leftmost lane, then return to the rightmost lane, and then stop. Meanwhile, other cars behave normally, drive a little faster, and switch lanes only in order to overtake other vehicles. These cars represent an obstacle for the buses to switch lanes.

Another advantage of dedicating the median area of the road to buses is having less emissions on sidewalks. The situation in Almaty is such that although the ecological problem is considered to be most important, there are a lot of buses that emit much more unburned gasoline than allowed. And even such a small distance would play a big role for pedestrians or cyclists.

The source codes can be found at: http://www.kuanysh.kz/revbus/source.zip

The binary can be found at: http://www.kuanysh.kz/revbus/release.zip

Moreover, Sect. 5.3 gives detailed information for the programmers.

2 Reversible Bus Lanes

A reversible lane is a lane in which traffic may flow in both directions, depending on time of the day or other conditions. Reversible lanes are used for optimizing traffic, mostly during rush hours. A good example is a connection of sleeping quarters and city centers. The flow to the city center in the morning is much stronger than in the opposite direction and is comparable to the flow to the sleeping quarters in the evening.

Reversible lane is a good solution when there is no space to widen the road any more because of buildings or in tunnels. Usually these lanes have a specially designed traffic lights to show the current direction. Otherwise some movable physical objects can be used for separating.

In our case we propose a reversible lane that is dedicated to only public transportation. It should forbid both directions twice a day for at least one hour for switching direction.

The question is why should this lane be forbidden to other vehicles? It could speed up the whole road, hence the buses would move faster even on right lanes. But the reality is that if this reversible lane is allowed to other traffic, it would not help in traffic jams. Frequent traffic jams in Kazakhstan are the main reason for introducing a separate lane for buses. On the other hand, this could stimulate some drivers use public transportation.

3   Simulation Conditions

Since the simulation depends on many circumstances, we assume the following facts:

1. The modeled system is a straight road that has no crossroads.
2. The speed of the cars is, on average, higher than the speed of the buses. Hence we decided that the maximum speed of the bus is 10 km/h less than the maximum speed of the cars. On the other hand, we only restrict the maximum speed, and the initial speed of both cars and buses is random, and it is changing throughout the simulation.
3. The acceleration (both positive and negative) is fixed to 7 km/h/sec for both cars and buses.
4. Buses do not slow down in order to switch the lane. We need the average distances that buses have to go in order to change to the reversible lane and back without forcing them to slow down.

4   Simulation Process

Obviously, we need to implement different algorithms for buses and cars. First of all, the main difference between them is their tactics for changing lanes. In case of cars, they may change lanes in order to outrun other cars. In case of buses they need to get to the leftmost lane as soon as possible and then return back to the rightmost lane for the bus stop. Theoretically, buses should drive on the reversible lane for longer, otherwise it is useless. But our goal is to show the very minimum distance between the bus stops so that introducing such lanes would make sense.

4.1   Changing Lanes

In order to fix the rules of the game, we need to introduce some definitions.

Definition 1. Minimal safe distance *of a car is a distance that the car travels in 0.3 s. This time is fixed intuitively by observing real cars in the city and can be changed by the "safeDistanceInSeconds" variable. So, the higher speed of the car is, the bigger minimal safe distance is.*

For example, for a car with the speed of 60 km/h, the minimal safe distance is 5 m. Note that if one needs to find the minimal safe distance between two cars then these 5 m include the length of the following car.

Definition 2. Emergency situation *is a condition when a car has to change its speed for avoiding collision with another car.*

An algorithm for changing of a car A to a lane L is as follows:

1. L is next to the current lane (left or right) and is not reversible.
2. The car is in an emergency situation, or there is no possibility to increase speed to its maximum.
3. There is no car or bus on lane L that is next to car A.
4. There is no car or bus on lane L that would become in an emergency situation or that would cause an emergency situation for car A, in case if A changes its lane to L.

Note that if a car is not in an emergency situation and is driving with the speed less than its maximum speed (each car has its own maximum speed) then it accelerates. See Sect. 4.4 for details.

An algorithm for buses movement is as follows:

1. The principles of safety while changing lanes are exactly the same as for cars (an emergency situation must not occur).
2. In case if the bus has never been to the reversible lane, it keeps movement and changes lane to the left one once it is safe.
3. In case if the bus has already been to the reversible lane, it keeps movement and changes lane to the right one once it is safe.
4. In case if the bus has been to the reversible lane and currently is on the rightmost lane, it slows down until full stop and then disappears.

4.2 Structures

We have implemented two structures in our project - Lane and Auto.

Lane structure represents one lane and has the following properties:

1. *isReverse*: Boolean variable, *True* if the lane is reversible.
2. *top*: Y-coordinate of the top of the lane.
3. *middle*: Y-coordinate of the middle of the lane.
4. *width*: The width of the lane.
5. *lastCarDistance*: Distance traveled so far by the last car on the lane. We use it to check whether there is enough space for a new car to appear.
6. *lastCarSpeed*: The speed of the last car on the lane.

Auto structure represents the class of vehicles (both cars and buses):

1. *isABus*: Boolean variable, *True* if the vehicle is a bus.
2. *lane*: Returns the number of the lane in order, starting from the right one (zero corresponds to the rightmost lane), on which the car currently is.
3. *passedDistance*: Distance traveled so far. This variable is responsible for the movement: increasing this value by 1 causes the vehicle move by 1 m. Note that the X-coordinate of the vehicle depends on *passedDistance* and the scale.
4. *length*: The length of the vehicle. This is random for each vehicle, but the buses are longer than cars.

5. *pictureId*: The number of the picture on screen that corresponds to the vehicle (rectangle index).
6. *hasCarInFront*: Boolean variable, *True* if there is a vehicle in front that causes slowing down.
7. *killed*: Boolean, *True* for all vehicles that are no longer in use.
8. *busReturning*: Boolean, *True* for all buses that have already been to the reversible lane, shows that the bus is returning to the rightmost lane. This variable is responsible for changing lanes.
9. *busTimer*: How long the bus is moving on the current lane. We use this variable to prevent the bus from changing two or more lanes at once. Moreover, it is natural for the drivers to have some interval between changing lanes.

4.3 Appearance of Cars and Buses

Vehicles should appear depending on the given traffic density. The user may fix the densities for the cars and buses separately before simulation starts. We have implemented so called caches for cars and buses that are responsible for the appearance of new vehicles. W.l.o.g., we will only show the algorithm for the appearance of cars. The principle of bus appearance is the same except of the initial speed: the cars start with their maximum speed, but the buses start with 0 km/h, as if they would start from the bus stop.

The buffer for the cars is called *carCache*. For simplicity reasons, we assume that the function (and other functions responsible for movement) is called once a second. In fact, it is called more frequently, depending on *animationSmoothness* variable that can be found in the program.

The appearance of a new car works as follows. If a new car (or several cars) should appear at some point in order to keep the traffic density, it does not appear immediately, but it goes to some buffer (*carCache* is incremented). Once any lane is free for a new vehicle, and the buffer is not empty, the vehicle is built, and *carCache* is decremented.

So, the *carCache* is updated as follows:

$$carCache = carCache + carsAnHour/60/60; \qquad (1)$$

I.e., if there should appear *carsAnHour* number of cars per hour, there should appear *carsAnHour*/60 cars per minute, and *carsAnHour*/60/60 cars per second.

Later, if *carsAnHour* ≥ 1, we call a function responsible for the creation of a new object. But before creating an object, we should find out which lane is the "most free" (if there is at least one free lane), and we should check whether we can reuse an old object, if it has *killed* = *True*.

In order to find the best lane for a new vehicle, we refresh the distances and speeds of the last cars on each lane. Once refreshed the distances, we search for the "best" lane for a new vehicle to appear by finding a lane with the maximum *lastCarDistance* value. And in case if such a lane exists (it may happen that all the lanes are busy), we create a new car with the following properties:

1. Maximum speed: 50 to 70 (random)
2. Car length: 4 ± 1 m (random, up to the centimeter)
3. Lane number: the above found lane
4. Speed: if the last car on the lane is moving with the speed less than the maximum speed of the new car, we take that last car's speed. Otherwise we take the maximum speed of the new car.

Note that if there is an old object that is not used any more, then the object is reused rather than creating a new one. This is done for performance reasons. Our first version of the program without reusing objects was very slow on some laptops after about 10 s of simulation.

4.4   Vehicle Movement Principles

The following algorithm updates logic for vehicles (again, w.l.o.g., once a second):

1. If the speed of the vehicle is less than the maximum, add 7 km./h.
2. Check if there is another vehicle in front with lower speed.
3. Check the safety of the distance to the vehicle in front (see Definition 1).
4. If the vehicle in front creates an emergency situation (see Definition 2), low down the speed and change to the neighbor lane when possible. Note that the lane change decision for buses is different (see Sect. 4.1).
5. If the bus has already been to the reversible lane, slow down. Once the speed of the bus is equal to zero, disappear.

5   Software Overview and Experiment Results

5.1   Software Overview

The software for our needs was written on C # and it represents several lanes for cars and a reversible lane for buses. W.l.o.g., we have simulated the traffic in only one direction as the opposite movement has no affect on the results.

After launching the program, the user has a chance to change some properties, like density of cars, density of buses, number of lanes (other than the reversible one). Note that the car density is set for all lanes, not for each lane. Hence, if one increases the number of lanes, the density on each lane will decrease.

On the picture below (Fig. 1), we can see yellow rectangles for buses and red rectangles for cars. In order to start simulation, the user has to fill in the fields "Number of cars/hour", "Number of buses/hour", and "Number of lanes". In the bottom of the window, we can see the statistics for 30 buses (513 m in average) .

5.2   Experiment Results

Our experiment was to try the simulation with different traffic density and different number of lanes. As mentioned above, the cars are simulated until they go too far (in this case 3 000 m), and the buses are simulated until they return to

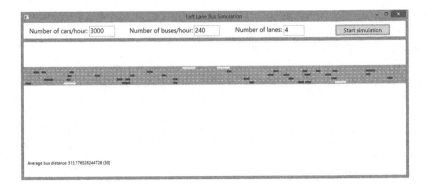

Fig. 1. Screenshot of the program

the rightmost lane and stop. There is one problem left unsolved when two buses are running with the same speed on neighbor lanes, so they can never change to each other's lane. This happens because in our model the buses never slow down to give a way to other vehicles.

On the picture below (Fig. 2) we can see three lines - the above line is the simulation with 4 lanes, the mid line is with 3 lanes, and the bottom line is with 2 lanes. The horizontal axis shows the number of vehicles per hour and the vertical axis shows the minimum bus stop distance.

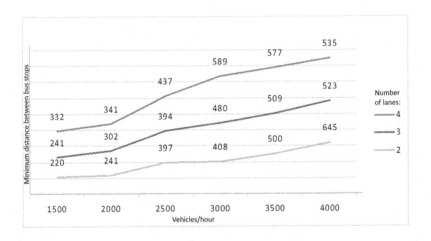

Fig. 2. Experiment results

We have simulated 30 buses for each experiment and calculated the average of all 30 buses. This way we have found the minimum distance between bus stops so that it would make sense to introduce such reversible lanes for buses.

5.3   Programming Details

This sections provides technical details on how this software functions. It could help understanding the source code and modify the software for ones needs.

The program is written in C# using WPF graphical subsystem. WPF uses the advantages of Direct X graphics device interface and has a very comfortable XAML language for designing user interfaces. The solution can be opened in Visual Studio 2012 or later.

Once Main Window is initialized, we initialize the timer that will be enabled once the user sets up all the properties and presses "Start simulation" button. Timer interval depends on the animationSmoothness and the speedFactor variables. Changing speedFactor variable will change the speed of the animation. But changing animationSmoothness will change only frames per second (the speed of the cars will be the same).

When the timer elapses, the following three functions are called: autoLogic, buildBuses, buildCars.

autoLogic function is responsible for all the logic of the program. This function works with each vehicle (current vehicle, midAuto) and does the following.

If the speed of the current vehicle is less than vehicle's maximum speed, we increase the speed by 7 km/h/animationSmoothness. Later we will check the speed and will decrease it if necessary. By now we force each vehicle to drive as fast as possible.

On the next step we check if there is any other vehicle in front of the current vehicle as follows. We take every vehicle ($auto[j]$) that is on the same lane

$$auto[j].lane == midAuto.lane,$$

in front of the current vehicle

$$auto[j].passedDistance > midAuto.passedDistance + midAuto.length,$$

too close to the current vehicle (depending on speed)

$$auto[j].passedDistance - midAuto.passedDistance - midAuto.length <$$
$$toMetersPerSecond(midAuto.speed) * safeDistanceInSeconds$$

and slow it down to the safe speed:

$$midAuto.speed = toKmPerHour((auto[j].passedDistance-$$
$$midAuto.passedDistance - midAuto.length)/safeDistanceInSeconds);$$

Here if there is such a car, we set the flag *hasCarInFront* to *True* in order to switch the lane when possible. This is the algorithm of changing lanes for cars.

For buses it is different. If a bus is on the same lane for more than 3 s, it should look for a chance to switch the lane. These three seconds guarantee that the bus will not switch more than one lane at a time. There is a variable *wishedLane* that defines the lane to which the bus should change next. It depends on whether the bus has already been to the reversible lane or not. Then we check if it is safe to change the lane by calling *laneIsFreeToSwitch* function. On the other hand, if *wishedLane* $= -1$, it means that the bus has been to the reversible lane and is already on the rightmost lane. Hence, this is time to stop now.

The function *laneIsFreeToSwitch* is also used by other cars in order to check whether it is safe to switch the lane, and if it returns *True*, the vehicle's *lane* variable is changed.

After all these manipulations with lane switching, it is time to change the positions of the vehicles. The position of each vehicle is determined by its lane number and the distance that was passed by the vehicle. The lane number was already changed before, so we now only change the *passedDistance* variable:

$$midAuto.passedDistance = midAuto.passedDistance+$$
$$toMetersPerSecond(midAuto.speed)/animationSmoothness;$$

In case if the passed distance is too big, we destroy the vehicle. Namely, we set the flag *killed* to *True* and increase the number of vehicles to be recycled. The first version of our program was deleting the object of the vehicle and then another object was created for the new vehicle. That version was very slow even on a modern desktop computer. The new version with reusing objects is fast even on most of the laptops.

Having updated the positions of each vehicle, we call *updateCarPicture* method for redrawing the rectangles.

buildBuses and *buildCars* functions are very similar, so we will concentrate on the *buildCars*. And since Sect. 4.3 describes the function detailed enough, we will only mention some deeper details that are not covered.

As we have mentioned before, this function is called every time timer elapses. And the interval of the timer depends on the number of frames we would like to display per second. Hence the function *buildCars* is called about, say, 50 times per second. Since we do not want to add vehicles so frequently, we count the number of calls (see Eq. 1 in Sect. 4.3):

$$carCache = carCache + carsAnHour/60/60/animationSmoothness;$$

This variable represents a buffer for the cars. If the cache becomes greater than one, this means that it is time to build one car. On the other hand, it may happen that the cache is even greater, this may happen if all the lanes are busy and there is no space for a new car. So the cache remembers how many cars are queued by now.

The animation part is pretty trivial. AnimationGrid represents a Grid control that holds all rectangles in Children collection. Each rectangle represents a vehicle and its width depends on the size of the car and the scale of the program. The scale can be chosen by changing *zoom* variable. AnimationGrid also holds several Line controls that represent the lane dividing lines.

6   Other Work

This experiment is a part of a bigger project named AutoSim for computer simulation of urban traffic. In this project we have developed a software for three-dimensional modeling of urban traffic using openstreetmap.org resources. The aim is to build a professional software with correspondence matrix, complicated calculations of emissions, etc. But as the first stage we aim to make a simple to use software for beginners in transportation, who could download any part of the world from openstreetmap.org and simulate it immediately without any fine-tuning. The problem of openstreetmap.org is that its map represents streets, not lanes. So we had to generate a lane-based map out of a streets map (see [6]). The hard part here is to come up with several lanes from each part of the street and connect them properly on crossroads. Some types of crossroads still presents a challenge for us.

Although AutoSim has quiet sophisticated algorithms for cars movement (changing lanes, accelerating, turning, finding shorter paths, etc.), nice looking cars, streets, houses, bridges, and trees, it still does not have any public transportation system like buses or trams. This has to be done in a later stage, and the results described in this paper will be used for lane changing decisions. We have faced some problems in this smaller project, that have to be solved before implementing buses in AutoSim.

Acknowledgments. We thank S. Badaev and K. Abeshev for the help, and the anonymous reviewers for useful suggestions. This work has been supported by the Ministry of Education of the Republic of Kazakhstan.

References

1. Valencia, A.: Modelo para planificación, operación y diseño físico de corredores de transporte público de superficie. M.Sc. thesis in Transport, Unversidad de Chile, Santiago (2008)
2. Valencia, A., Fernandez, R.: Macroscopic simulation approach of public transport on exclusive lanes. In: European Transport Conference (2011)
3. Chen, X., Cai, P., Zhu, L., Yu, L.: Micro-simulation study of the effect of median bus lanes with midblock stop on capacity of urban signalized intersection. In: 2010 13th International IEEE Conference on Intelligent Transportation Systems (ITSC), 19–22 September 2010, pp. 1033–1038 (2010)
4. Ilahi, A., Irawan, M.Z.: A microsimulation model of median busway and ATCS (case study: Transjogja Bus, Yogyakarta, Indonesia). In: Proceedings of the Eastern Asia Society for Transportation Studies, vol. 9 (2013)
5. Fernandez, R.: A new approach to bus stop modelling. Traffic Eng. Control **42**(7), 240–246 (2001)
6. Bakibayev, T., Abeshyev, K.: Adaptation of GIS Open Source Maps to Lanes Graph. Karagandy State University, No. 04 (72) (2013). http://www.ksu.kz/files/Vestnik_KSU/Mathematics_4_72_2013.pdf

A Combinatorial Approach to Knot Recognition

Andrew Fish[1], Alexei Lisitsa[2], and David Stanovský[3,4](✉)

[1] School of Computing, Engineering and Mathematics,
University of Brighton, Brighton, UK
[2] Department of Computer Science, The University of Liverpool, Liverpool, UK
[3] Department of Information Systems and Mathematical Modeling,
International IT University, Almaty, Kazakhstan
[4] Department of Algebra, Faculty of Mathematics and Physics,
Charles University, Prague, Czech Republic
stanovsk@karlin.mff.cuni.cz

Abstract. This is a report on our ongoing research on a combinatorial approach to knot recognition, using coloring of knots by certain algebraic objects called quandles. The aim of the paper is to summarize the mathematical theory of knot coloring in a compact, accessible manner, and to show how to use it for computational purposes. In particular, we address how to determine colorability of a knot, and propose to use SAT solving to search for colorings. The computational complexity of the problem, both in theory and in our implementation, is discussed. In the last part, we explain how coloring can be utilized in knot recognition.

1 Introduction

Knot recognition is a central problem in computational knot theory. Given two *knots* (closed loops in space without self-intersection), or rather their descriptions (such as their diagrams, Gauss codes, etc.), are they *equivalent* in the sense that there is an ambient isotopy (informally, a continuous deformation of space) transforming one knot into the other?

Although it all started with Kelvin's hypothesis that different elements are differently knotted vortices of ether [20], most of the work on knot recognition is a typical mathematical endeavour, with little care paid to potential applications. Nevertheless, current real life motivation to study knots exist: for example, some molecules, such as DNA, can occur knotted, and their chemical or biological properties depend on the way they are knotted (it is reported that certain antibiotics exploit topological properties of DNA). See [1, Sect. 7] or [4] for details and other applications of knots in biology, chemistry and physics.

Knot theory, since its beginnings in late 19th century, has used mostly geometric and topological methods, often supported by an algebraic framework (algebraic topology, homological algebra, polynomials). This is somewhat surprising, since tame knots can be considered as finite graph-like structures (see [18] for more ideas in this direction); the tameness condition is imposed to rule out

D. Stanovský—Partially supported by the GAČR grant 13-01832S.

R. Horne (Ed.): EGC 2015, CCIS 514, pp. 64–78, 2015.
DOI: 10.1007/978-3-319-25043-4_7

pathological cases. An entirely new approach appeared in foundational papers by Joyce [12] and Matveev [17] where certain algebraic structures, called *quandles*, were introduced and used to obtain a complete invariant (up to reverse mirroring), called the knot quandle. While their motivation was to capture the essential part of the knot group, their works paved the way to introduce an extensive class of combinatorial knot invariants, based on coloring of arcs by (finite) quandles.

The present paper is an initial report on our project to turn the coloring method into a practical computational tool for knot recognition. In the first part (Sect. 3), we summarize the mathematical theory necessary to understand the algorithms. The ideas are old, but dispersed around various sources; our contribution is a compact self-contained presentation of the material. Then, we discuss how to find a coloring, computationally. A theoretical framework and the complexity of the problem is addressed in Sect. 4.1. To search for a coloring in practice, we propose to use SAT solving. This idea seems to be new and our initial experiments are reported in detail in Sect. 4.2 which is the core of the paper. In the last part, we explain how coloring can be utilized for knot recognition (Sect. 5), building upon earlier ideas of [6,8].

Readers not familiar with basic notions of knot theory are recommended to take a fine crash course on Wikipedia[1]. A standard textbook reference is [1]. By an *unknot* we mean any knot equivalent to the trivial knot, a simple circle in space. Informally, unknots are knots that can be untangled. Non-specialists are recommended to read the article [10] to learn what is so hard about unknotting unknots.

All knots in the text are assumed to be tame and oriented. For computational purposes, knots are presented in the form of diagrams, which are regular planar projections, so that the only singularities of the projection are transverse double points, and these bear additional information about the relative height of strands at every crossing. The size of a knot diagram then refers to the number of crossings, which determines, for instance, the size of its Gaussian code or other diagram encodings. Greek letters α, β, γ will be used for knot arcs, and latin letters a, b, c for colors.

2 Classical Approach to Knot Recognition

Mathematicians have been working on the knot recognition problem for more than a century, yet are nowhere near a satisfactory solution. The standard approach is based on calculating *invariants*, properties shared by equivalent knots. Classical invariants use various algebraic constructions to code some of the topological properties of a knot. Typical examples are polynomial invariants, for instance:

– The *Alexander polynomial*. It can distinguish most small knots, yet there are infinitely many knots with trivial Alexander polynomial (hence indistinguishable from the unknots). A polynomial time algorithm, fast in practice, exists (based on calculation of a determinant of a sparse matrix).

---

[1] http://en.wikipedia.org/wiki/Knot_theory.

- The *Jones polynomial* and several common generalizations of the Jones and Alexander polynomials. They tend to distinguish even more knots, yet it is not known whether they distinguish unknots. Better performance comes for a price: calculating (or even approximating) the Jones polynomial is known to be #P-hard.
- The currently fashionable *Khovanov homology* is the "categorification" of the Jones polynomial. It provably distinguishes unknots, but is even harder to calculate in practice.

Among other classical methods, let us mention the *knot group*, the fundamental group of the knot complement, which informally describes the "holes" the knot creates in space. While fairly powerful in theory (for instance, it does distinguish unknots), it is not directly useful for calculations, since there is no algorithm to handle the isomorphism problem for finitely presented groups.

From what we have said so far, it would not even be clear whether knot recognition is algorithmically decidable. However, it was shown to be decidable by Haken in 1962, by an algorithm which was considered impractical for implementation. The complexity of knot recognition is an interesting and widely open problem.

Even the special case of *unknot recognition* (formally, given a knot, is it equivalent to an unknot?) is not fully understood, although there has been significant progress over the past 20 years. At the moment, unknot recognition is known to be both in the NP and coNP complexity classes (coNP assuming the Generalized Riemann Hypothesis, GRH). A polynomial-time checkable certificate of unknottedness was found by Hass, Lagarias and Pippenger [9], using the theory of normal surfaces. A more natural certificate, a polynomial length sequence of Reidemeister moves that untangles an unknot, has been conjectured for a long time, but was only proved to exist by Lackenby [15] very recently (however, it provides no clue for how to find that short sequence efficiently). On the other hand, a polynomial-time certificate for knottedness was proved to exist by Kuperberg [14], assuming GRH, taking the Kronheimer-Mrówka representation of the knot group over the group $SL(2, \mathbb{C})$ and using GRH to project it to a representation over a finite field of a sufficiently small size.

3   Combinatorial Approach to Knot Recognition

A combinatorial approach to knot theory is possible, following Reidemeister, since two knots are ambient isotopic if and only if they have diagrams which differ by a finite sequence of local diagram rewrite rules called Reidemeister moves. Thus, invariants of knots can be constructed as invariants of knot diagrams which do not change under the Reidemeister moves.

3.1   Coloring Knots

One of the first invariants ever considered was *tricolorability*: color the arcs of a knot diagram with three colors in a way that, at every crossing, the three strands have either the same, or three different colors. Every knot admits three *trivial colorings*, with all arcs painted in the same color. A knot diagram is called tricolorable if it admits a non-trivial tricoloring. It is not difficult to show that tricolorability is invariant with respect to Reidemeister moves, and so it is a property of knots (not just their diagrams) which is invariant with respect to knot equivalence. More generally, the number of non-trivial tricolorings of a knot K, $col_3(K)$, is an invariant.

Fig. 1. Tricolored trefoil and five-colored figure-eight (Color figure online).

Figure 1 shows an example of a non-trivial tricoloring. Tricolorability is not a terribly good invariant: for instance, it cannot distinguish the figure-eight knot from an unknot, as the figure-eight knot admits no non-trivial tricoloring.

More generally, one can consider *Fox n-colorings*, using colors $0, 1, \ldots, n-1$, and the rule that, for every crossing, the sum of the colors of the two lower strands equals twice the color of the bridge, modulo n. The number $col_n(K)$ of non-trivial n-colorings is an invariant, which is easily calculated using linear algebra and the Chinese Remainder Theorem. Figure 1 shows an example of a non-trivial 5-coloring of the figure-eight knot (only four colors are used, but, importantly, the arithmetic is modulo 5). Notice that Fox 3-coloring is the same thing as tricoloring.

Fig. 2. Labeled crossing.

There is an common framework for these and other arc coloring invariants. Let C be a set (of colors) and $*$ a binary operation on C. A *coloring* of a knot diagram is a mapping f assigning to every arc a color from C in a manner that, for every crossing with arcs labeled α, β, γ as in Fig. 2, the equation

$$f(\alpha) * f(\beta) = f(\gamma) \tag{E}$$

is satisfied. A coloring is called trivial if it only uses one color. For example, tricolorability uses a set C with $|C| = 3$ and the operation defined by $a * a = a$

for every $a \in C$ and $a * b$ equal to the third color whenever $a \neq b$. Fox n-coloring uses $C = \{0, 1, \ldots, n-1\}$ and $a * b = 2a - b \bmod n$.

Let $\text{col}_Q(D)$ denote the number of non-trivial colorings of the knot diagram D by the algebraic structure $Q = (C, *)$. Not every algebraic structure provides an invariant. The following theorem determines such instances.

Theorem 1. *Let $Q = (C, *)$ be an algebraic structure over a set C with a binary operation $*$ satisfying the following conditions for every $a, b, c \in C$:*

(1) $a * a = a$ (idempotence);
(2) there is a unique $x \in C$ such that $a * x = b$ (unique left division);
(3) $a * (b * c) = (a * b) * (a * c)$ (left self-distributivity).

Then col_Q is a knot invariant.

The algebraic structures satisfying conditions (1), (2), (3) are called *quandles*. (We use the *left* notation for quandles.)

Theorem 1 is a consequence of the theory developed in [12, 17]. Here is a sketch of the direct proof.

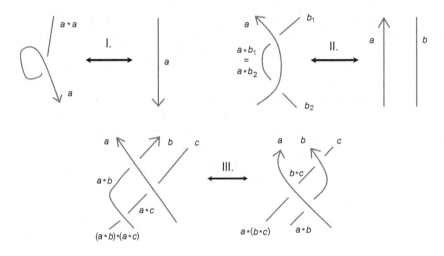

Fig. 3. Reidemeister moves and invariance of coloring (Color figure online).

It is sufficient to show that col_Q is invariant with respect to the three Reidemeister moves, i.e., if two diagrams D, D' differ by a single move, the number of non-trivial colorings remains the same. We prove that every coloring of D corresponds uniquely to a coloring of D' that uses identical colors for arcs outside the scope of the move, including those crossing the move's borderline.

For the type I move, there are two options for the orientation. For the downwards orientation as in Fig. 3, assume the color of the lower arc in the lefthand picture is a. Then, the color of the upper arc is $a * a$. Using (1), we have $a * a = a$, hence every coloring of the lefthand diagram colors both arcs in the same color, and thus corresponds to a unique coloring of the righthand diagram. For the upwards orientation, the upper arc has a color x such that $a * x = a$. Using (2), this color is uniquely determined, and using (1), $x = a$, and the same argument proves the case.

For the type II move, there are two options for the orientation, again. For the upwards orientation as in Fig. 3, assume the colors of the border arcs in the lefthand picture are a, b_1, b_2, respectively. Then, the color of the middle arc is $a * b_1 = a * b_2$, hence uniquely determined by a, b_1, b_2. Moreover, using (2), we have $b_1 = b_2$. Hence every coloring of the lefthand diagram corresponds to a uniquely determined coloring of the righthand diagram. Thanks to (1), non-trivial colorings correspond mutually. A similar argument proves the downwards orientation.

For the type III move as in Fig. 3, assume the colors of the top arcs be a, b, c, respectively. The colors of the remaining arcs are uniquely determined as in the picture. To obtain the same color for the left bottom arc, we use condition (3). For the other three orientations, we proceed similarly; condition (2) is needed for unique solutions as in case I.

Looking at the proof sketch, we see that the three axioms of quandles relate very well to the three Reidemeister moves. Invariance with respect to type II moves uses precisely condition (2), and invariance with respect to types I and III moves uses precisely conditions (1) and (3), respectively, in some cases under the assumption of unique left division. The converse statement, that *quandles are the only structures providing arc coloring invariants of knots*, is also true in certain way, but the precise statement and a proof is beyond the scope of the present paper.

3.2   Quandles

A natural question arises: what really are quandles? The answer is not yet fully understood, but in the most important case, of so called *algebraically connected quandles*, it is. We will briefly summarize the theory in the next paragraph. Readers with no background in group theory can safely skip it and continue reading about the examples of quandles below.

A quandle $Q = (C, *)$ is algebraically connected if the permutation group generated by the left translations $L_a(x) = a * x$ is transitive on C. It is not difficult to prove that colors used in a coloring generate an algebraically connected subquandle [19, Sect. 5.2], hence, without loss of generality, we can consider only Q-colorings with a connected Q. Such quandles were studied in detail in several papers, the strongest results were obtained recently in [11]. The main theorem states that connected quandles are in 1-1 correspondence to certain configurations in transitive groups: every connected quandle on a set C is uniquely determined by a pair (G, ζ) where G is a transitive group on C and ζ is a central element of the stabilizer G_e such that $\langle \zeta^G \rangle = G$ (uniqueness up to the choice of e); an isomorphism theorem is available. Using the theory of [11], and a library of transitive groups of degree n, one can easily enumerate all connected quandles of size n up to isomorphism. Currently, such a library is available for $n \leq 47$.

Let us introduce three important classes of quandles.

A quandle $Q = (C, *)$ is called *affine* if there is an abelian group $G = (C, +)$ (informally, an addition on the set of colors) and an automorphism φ such that $a * b = a - \varphi(a) + \varphi(b)$ for every $a, b \in C$ (informally, $*$ is an affine combination of colors). For example, Fox n-coloring uses the affine quandle with $G = \mathbb{Z}_n$ and $\varphi(x) = -x$. An affine quandle is connected if and only if the mapping $x \mapsto x - \varphi(x)$ is onto.

Given a group G and a conjugacy class C in G, then $(C, *)$ with $a * b = aba^{-1}$ is called a *conjugation quandle* over G. Conjugation quandles may or may not be connected.

A quandle is called *simple* if it has no proper homomorphic images (other than itself and the trivial one). Finite simple quandles with $|C| > 2$ are always connected and were characterized in [2,13]: they are either affine, or arise from a finite simple group using a sort of parametrized conjugation operation on its orbit of transitivity; the construction can be used to create a large list of simple quandles. Within the framework of [11] (see the description above), simple quandles are recognized as those where every factor of G is cyclic and the centralizer of ζ is contained in G_e [2]; the message is that it is computationally easy to verify whether a given quandle is simple.

3.3 Colorability and Simple Quandles

If $col_Q(K) > 0$, we say that the knot K is *Q-colorable*. Now, Q-colorability is also an invariant, which is easier to calculate than $col_Q(K)$: one only has to establish that $col_Q(K) > 0$, whereas the actual number of colorings, $col_Q(K)$, is often rather big due to the high symmetry of quandles [6], and finding all of them can be computationally costly.

The following observation suggests that if we only care about colorability (and not the actual number of colorings), we can restrict to simple quandles.

Lemma 1. *Let K be a knot which is colorable by a finite quandle Q. Then K is colorable by a finite simple quandle Q' such that $|Q'| \leq |Q|$.*

Proof. Consider a non-trivial coloring f of K by Q. Let Q'' be the subquandle of Q generated by all colors used in the coloring f. Indeed, f is a coloring of K by Q''. Let α be a maximal congruence of Q''. Then the factor, $Q' = Q''/\alpha$, is a finite simple quandle (because α is maximal). Consider the composition $f' = \pi \circ f$ where π is the natural projection $Q'' \to Q'$. Then f' is a non-trivial coloring of K by Q'. Equation (E) follows from the fact that π is a homomorphism: for every crossing as in Fig. 2, $f'(\alpha) * f'(\beta) = \pi(f(\alpha)) * \pi(f(\beta)) = \pi(f(\alpha) * f(\beta)) = \pi(f(\gamma)) = f'(\gamma)$. If f' was trivial, then all colors used by f were in one block, B, of α. Since congruence blocks are subquandles and Q'' is generated by all such colors, $B = Q''$, hence α was the total congruence $Q'' \times Q''$, a contradiction.

4   Finding a Coloring

Given a quandle Q and a knot K, a natural question is "how do we calculate $\mathrm{col}_Q(K)$, the number of non-trivial Q-colorings?" For simplicity, let us focus on the decision problem of Q-colorability: "does there exists a non-trivial Q-coloring of K?", i.e. can we decide if $\mathrm{col}_Q(K) > 0$. We will always assume a knot K is presented as a diagram, and we let $|K|$ denote the number of crossings of the diagram.

4.1   Theory

Naturally, this problem is in the complexity class NP: given an assignment of colors to arcs, it is easy to check whether it is a non-trivial Q-coloring. To find a coloring, one has to solve a system of equations over the quandle Q: for every crossing as in Fig. 2, we have the equation $x_\alpha * x_\beta = x_\gamma$, where $x_\alpha, x_\beta, x_\gamma$ are variables that determine the colors of the arcs α, β, γ. This can be viewed as an instance of the Constraint Satisfaction Problem (CSP): arcs are variables, Q is the domain, and the equations are the constraints. In general, CSP is an NP-complete problem (SAT is a special instance of CSP). But how hard are the knot coloring instances? In particular, how hard is Q-colorability for a fixed quandle Q? How hard is Q-colorability for a fixed knot K?

One can try a simple brute force search: to every one of $|K|$ arcs, assign one of $|Q|$ colors, and check whether this is a non-trivial coloring; we are handling $|Q|^{|K|}$ assignments. For a fixed knot K, this gives a polynomial time algorithm with respect to $|Q|$, but this is impractical for larger knots. Can we do with a better exponent than $|K|$?

Given a braid representation of K, with n strands (the smallest possible n is called the *braid index* of K), the brute force search is only required to assign colors to the initial n arcs, since the colors of the remaining arcs are uniquely determined; hence, we only handle $|Q|^n$ assignments. Whilst this provides a dramatic improvement in practice, the algorithm is still exponential-time with respect to $|K|$ (leaving aside conversion into braid representation). See [6] for a more detailed description and experimental results.

Universal algebra provides a different point of view on coloring. We are solving a system of $|K|$ equations over the quandle Q. The complexity of equation solving over general algebraic structures has been studied extensively. In our case, it follows from general results of Larose and Zádori [16] that the problem of solving a general system of equations over a quandle Q is polynomial-time if and only if Q is affine, and it is NP-complete otherwise. Consequently, colorability by affine quandles (and Fox coloring in particular) is easy. Nevertheless, it does not mean that colorability by non-affine quandles is hard, because the systems of equations arising from knot coloring have a very special form! It is an interesting open problem whether a polynomial time algorithm for Q-colorability exists for every quandle Q.

We are not aware of any other theoretical results applicable to the complexity of quandle colorings.

4.2 Practice

The only attempt to calculate quandle colorings on a larger scale we know about
is reported in [6]. Their implementation was tested on all knots with at most 12
crossings, their performance graph exhibits a fast growth of running time with
respect to $|Q|$.

We propose a more efficient approach to knot coloring: a reduction to the
Boolean Satisfiability Problem, SAT. Fix a connected quandle $Q = (\{1, \ldots, q\}, *)$
and a knot diagram K with $|K| = n$, with arcs numbered $\alpha_1, \ldots, \alpha_n$. We consider
nq boolean variables $v_{i,c}$ that determine whether the arc α_i has the color c. We
need to satisfy the following constraints:

- Every arc has a unique color: the obvious description uses the clauses

$$v_{i,1} \vee \ldots \vee v_{i,q} \quad \text{and} \quad \neg v_{i,c} \vee \neg v_{i,d}$$

  for every $i = 1, \ldots, n$ and $c = 1, \ldots, q$, $d = c+1, \ldots, q$.
- Not all arcs have the same color: the obvious description uses, for every
  $c = 1, \ldots, q$, the clause

$$\neg v_{1,c} \vee \ldots \vee \neg v_{n,c}.$$

- Crossing equations (E): for every crossing, with a bridge α_i over the strands
  α_j to the right and α_k to the left, we use q^2 formulas of the form

$$(v_{i,c} \wedge v_{j,d}) \rightarrow v_{k,c*d}.$$

An important ingredient is basic symmetry breaking: since connected quandles are homogeneous, we can assume that the arc α_1 has color 1. (If we were
counting the number of colorings, and not just checking colorability, then we
could recover $\text{col}_Q(K)$ by multiplying the answer by $|Q|$).

We implemented the procedure, employing a standard SAT-solver MiniSat
1.14. For our experiments, we used the family

SQ. of all 354 simple quandles of size ≤ 47, indexed in accordance to size,

(the reason is explained in Lemma 1); and the following three families of knots:

12A. all 1288 alternating knots with crossing number 12 (taken from [5]),
  T2. $(2, n)$-torus knots with $n = 11, 21, 31, \ldots, 91$,
  T3. $(3, n)$-torus knots with $n = 14, 20, 26, \ldots, 98$.

(Torus knots are some of the best known and easiest to implement, potentially
infinite, families of knots.) Figs. 4–7 present performance graphs with respect to
various parameters.

First of all, we must stress that neither the number of crossings, nor the
braid index, are the most relevant knot parameters with respect to running time.
Figure 4 shows the distribution of running times for the family **12A**. Whilst most
knots are colored quickly, there are several "slow" knots, with the record being
held by the knot with KnotInfo [5] code 12a_1092, see Fig. 8. We were unable to

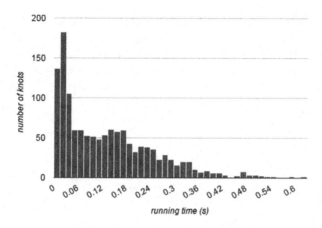

Fig. 4. Distribution of running times (in seconds) for the **12A** family, averaged over all quandles in **SQ**.

identify any possible reason that makes this particular knot harder than others. Also notice the high noisiness of the performance graphs for the $(3, n)$-torus knots in Fig. 5. Yet again, it is not merely the number of crossings that determines the running time.

For the **T3** family, the average running time fluctuates more than the median running time. This suggests that the peaks are caused by a few very long computations, while a "random" coloring job runs relatively fast. For example, for the $(3, 92)$-torus knot, which is the last but one node on the right graph in Fig. 5, the running times for most quandles are no more than a few seconds, but the few exceptions run for a few hundreds of seconds. Perhaps this is an indication that while it is fast to determine Q-colorability on average, it could be hard in the worst case.

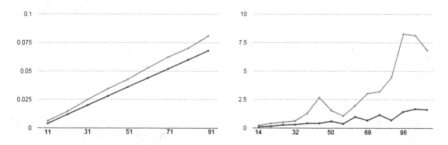

Fig. 5. Average (red, top line) and median (blue, bottom line) running times (s) over all quandles in **SQ**, with respect to knot size for knots in **T2** (on the left) and **T3** (on the right), respectively (Color figure online).

Both graphs in Fig. 5 suggest that the dependence of median running time with respect to knot size is roughly linear for torus knots. This is not surprising, and probably far from the general case because (k, n)-torus knots have a fixed braid index k, for every n, and so a brute force search in the spirit of [6] runs in linear time with respect to n, by choosing k initial colors and running along the torus producing the remaining coloring values. Nevertheless, in the **T3** case, it seems the SAT solver has a hard time to recognize the braids, and therefore, the running times fluctuate.

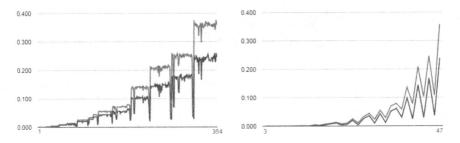

Fig. 6. Average (red, top line) and median (blue, bottom line) running times (s) over knots in **12A**, with respect to quandle index (on the left), and quandle size (on the right), respectively (Color figure online).

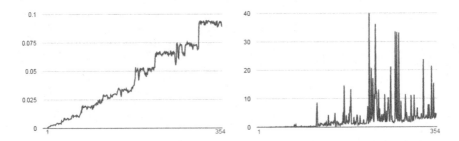

Fig. 7. Average running times (s) over knots in **T2** (on the left) and **T3** (on the right), respectively, with respect to quandle index.

The graphs in Figs. 6 and 7 indicate the time complexity with respect to quandle index and quandle size (by index, we mean the position in the list **SQ**). Looking at the lefthand graphs, addressing the **12A** and **T2** knots, we observe a staircase behavior. It tells that quandles of equal size have similar running times. For **12A** knots, we observe occasional deep drops. These are precisely the positions of non-affine quandles, which are, on average, much faster than the affine ones. This is somewhat surprising, since, in theory, non-affine quandles are the harder ones (see Sect. 4.1). The reason might be a higher symmetry of affine quandles, invisible to MiniSat, together with its inability to employ the fast coloring algorithm.

For **T3** knots (Fig. 7, right), the situation is different: the graph is much noisier and the majority of the peaks are at non-affine positions. While non-affine quandles seem faster in "random" cases, they also provide the majority of very long running times.

Observing the growth of running time with respect to quandle index, we see it is somewhat faster than linear, but certainly subquadratic. What about the dependence with respect to quandle size, $|Q|$? Since the number of simple quandles of size n appears to grow roughly linearly with n (this is only an empirical observation based on the family **SQ**, we have no formal arguments yet), we shall add one to the degree. Figure 6 confirms the idea. Since all affine simple quandles have prime power size, and all non-affine simple quandles have size divisible by at least two primes, the right graph reflects the drops and peaks of the left graph.

We can draw the following conclusion. Even a simple implementation, using an obsolete solver and no fine tuning, is competitive, outperforming the brute-force search considerably. Our programs and computation data are available at our website[2].

5   Recognizing Knots and Unknots

5.1   Proving Inequivalence

Let K_1, K_2 be two knots. If we find a quandle Q such that $\mathrm{col}_Q(K_1) \neq \mathrm{col}_Q(K_2)$ (or, in particular, such that K_1 is Q-colorable and K_2 is not), we can conclude that K_1 and K_2 are not equivalent. Large libraries of connected quandles can be created using the methods described in Sect. 3.2. For instance, it is feasible to compile the complete list of connected quandles up to size 47, the complete list of conjugation quandles over any group with hundreds of elements, the complete list of affine quandles of any size in the order of thousands.

An interesting experiment is described in [6]. All knots with at most 12 crossings can be distinguished (up to mirror image) using a list of 26 finite quandles, the largest having 182 elements. Most pairs of knots are distinguished using a fairly small quandle, and therefore relatively quickly. More details and other interesting findings can be found in [6].

Unfortunately, no upper bound is known for the size of a quandle that distinguishes two inequivalent knots, and it is not even known whether a finite quandle is sufficient. In particular, it is not known whether coloring provides a decision procedure for knot recognition.

5.2   Recognizing Unknots

In [8], the first two named authors proposed to use automated theorem proving on knot quandles for unknot recognition, i.e., for the decision of whether a given knot is equivalent to an unknot. Here we present the idea in terms a quandle

---

[2] http://www.karlin.mff.cuni.cz/~stanovsk/quandles.

coloring in a somewhat reshaped manner. The method is based on Theorem 2, which is collected from several works.

Theorem 2. *The following are equivalent for a knot K:*

(1) K is knotted (i.e., not an unknot).
(2) There is a quandle Q such that $\mathrm{col}_Q(K) > 0$.
(3) There is a finite quandle Q such that $\mathrm{col}_Q(K) > 0$.
(4) There is a finite simple quandle Q such that $\mathrm{col}_Q(K) > 0$.
(5) There is a conjugation quandle Q over the group $SL(2, p)$, for a prime p, such that $\mathrm{col}_Q(K) > 0$.

The equivalence of (1) and (2) was proved in [12,17]. The equivalence of (2) and (3) was proved in [7]. The equivalence of (3) and (4) follows from Lemma 1. The equivalence of (1) and (5) is a translation of Kuperberg's certificate of knottedness [14] into the language of quandles (this part of Kuperberg's result is independent of GRH which is only needed to guarantee that p is small enough). Notice that the implication (2) ⇒ (1) follows from Theorem 1: the trivial knot has only one arc, hence admits only trivial colorings; since col_Q is an invariant, so does any unknot.

Theorem 2 turns quandle coloring into a decision procedure for unknot recognition: given a knot on input, we run two independent algorithms (ideally in parallel), one seeking for a certificate of knottedness, the other for unknotting. For knottedness, it is sufficient to find a non-trivial coloring; condition (3) says it is sufficient to consider finite colorings, and conditions (4) and (5) suggest particular families of finite quandles to try. For unknottedness, it is sufficient to *prove* that no non-trivial coloring exists, and automated theorem proving provides a tool to do so.

Detailed experiments with the proposed decision procedure will be reported in a subsequent paper. To certify knottedness, for example, the family **SQ** of simple quandles of size ≤ 47 is sufficient for all **12A** knots and for many larger knots. Certification running times are competitive against state-of-the-art in knot recognition. The unknottedness certification has been tested on various famous "hard unknots" with a positive outcome, see [8] for details.

Fig. 8. Tricolored knot with KnotInfo [5] code 12a_1092 (Color figure online).

Efficience of the knottedness certification heavily relies on efficiency of the coloring procedure used. Nevertheless, for a particular knot, the complexity of the two problems seems to be related only loosely: for example, the slowest knot reported in Sect. 4.2 is tricolorable (see Fig. 8), hence certified very quickly.

5.3   Classic Vs. Combinatorial

We believe that many classical results in knot theory can be explained in terms of coloring, perhaps in a more systematic or conceptually cleaner form. A few sample results can be found in [6, Sect. 7]. A different kind of example has been mentioned earlier in our paper: Kuperberg's certificate of knottedness is a prime p and a non-commutative representation of the knot group over $SL(2, p)$, which is the same thing as a non-trivial coloring by a conjugation quandle over $SL(2, p)$ (the Wirtinger presentation of the knot group uses arcs as generators and conjugation relations analogous to condition (E) for every crossing).

Here is another, perhaps more important, example. The Alexander invariant is essentially the same thing as coloring by affine quandles. We refer to [3] for a precise statement, and we state formally a result related to Theorem 2.

Theorem 3. *The following are equivalent for a knot K.*

(1) K has a non-trivial Alexander polynomial.
(3) There is a finite affine quandle Q such that $\mathrm{col}_Q(K) > 0$.
(4) There is a finite simple affine quandle Q such that $\mathrm{col}_Q(K) > 0$.

The theorem can be used to considerably improve efficiency of search for inequivalence certificates. Let K_1, K_2 be two knots. First, we calculate their Alexander polynomials Δ_1, Δ_2 (a fast algorithm exists). If $\Delta_1 \neq \Delta_2$, the knots are inequivalent. Else, continue as before. If we only test for Q-colorability (such as in the knottedness certificate described in the previous subsection), we can exclude all affine quandles from the search. This can result in a considerable cut of the search space: for instance, out of the 354 simple quandles with at most 47 elements, only 23 are non-affine.

6   Conclusion

We presented a new approach to knot recognition, based on coloring the arcs of a knot by certain algebraic objects. Unlike most of the classical invariants, finding a coloring is a combinatorial problem, amenable to a (smart) exhaustive search. The coloring method is provably a decision procedure for recognizing unknots, and works very well in practice for general knot recognition, too. In both cases, most instances of inequivalence are certified very quickly.

The obvious future work is a careful analysis of the parameters of the decision procedure (efficient SAT encoding, choice of the quandle family, heuristics in the spirit of Theorem 3) to improve efficiency of knottedness certification in practice. To extend the method towards general knot recognition, a generalization of Theorem 2 is much needed.

References

1. Adams, C.: The Knot Book: An Elementary Introduction to the Mathematical Theory of Knots. Amer. Math. Soc., Providence (1994)
2. Andruskiewitsch, N., Graña, M.: From racks to pointed Hopf algebras. Adv. Math. **178**(2), 177–243 (2003)
3. Bae, Y.: Coloring link diagrams by Alexander Quandles. J. Knot Theory Ramifications **21**(10), 1250094 (2012)
4. Buck, D., Flapan, E. (eds.): Applications of Knot Theory. Proceedings of Symposia in Applied Mathematics. Amer. Math. Soc., Providence (2009)
5. Cha, J.C., Livingston, C.: KnotInfo: Table of knot invariants. http://www.indiana.edu/~knotinfo
6. Clark, W.E., Elhamdadi, M., Saito, M., Yeatman, T.: Quandle colorings of knots and applications. J. Knot Theory Ramifications **23**(6), 1450035 (2014)
7. Clark, W.E., Saito, M., Vendramin, L.: Quandle coloring and cocycle invariants of composite knots and abelian extensions. http://arxiv.org/abs/1407.5803
8. Fish, A., Lisitsa, A.: Detecting unknots via equational reasoning, I: Exploration. In: Watt, S.M., Davenport, J.H., Sexton, A.P., Sojka, P., Urban, J. (eds.) CICM 2014. LNCS, vol. 8543, pp. 76–91. Springer, Heidelberg (2014)
9. Hass, J., Lagarias, J., Pippenger, N.: The computational complexity of knot and link problems. J. ACM **46**, 185–211 (1999)
10. Henrich, A., Kauffman, L.: Unknotting Unknots. Am. Math. Monthly **121**(5), 379–390 (2014)
11. Hulpke, A., Stanovský, D., Vojtěchovský, P.: Connected quandles and transitive groups. To appear in J. Pure Appl. Algebra. http://arxiv.org/abs/1409.2249
12. Joyce, D.: Classifying invariant of knots, the knot quandle. J. Pure Appl. Algebra **23**, 37–65 (1982)
13. Joyce, D.: Simple quandles. J. Algebra **79**, 307–318 (1982)
14. Kuperberg, G.: Knottedness is in NP, modulo GRH. Adv. Math. **256**, 493–506 (2014)
15. Lackenby, M.: A polynomial upper bound on Reidemeister moves. To appear in Annals Math. http://arxiv.org/abs/1302.0180
16. Larose, B., Zádori, L.: Taylor terms, constraint satisfaction and the complexity of polynomial equations over finite algebras. Internat. J. Algebra Comput. **16**(3), 563–581 (2006)
17. Matveev, S.V.: Distributive groupoids in knot theory. Math. USSR - Sbornik **47**(1), 73–83 (1984)
18. Nelson, S.: The combinatorial revolution in knot theory. Notices Amer. Math. Soc. **58**(11), 1553–1561 (2011)
19. Ohtsuki, T.: Problems on Invariants of Knots and 3-manifolds. Geom. Topol. Monogr., vol. 4. Geom. Topol. Publ., Coventry (2002)
20. Silver, D.S.: Knot theory's odd origins. Am. Sci. **94**, 158–165 (2006)

MultiBox: Lightweight Containers for Vendor-Independent Multi-cloud Deployments

James Hadley[(✉)], Yehia Elkhatib, Gordon Blair, and Utz Roedig

Lancaster University, Lancaster LA1 4WA, UK
j.hadley1@lancaster.ac.uk

Abstract. Cloud computing aims to make a large selection of sophisticated technologies available to users for deployment and migration. In reality, once a cloud service provider has been chosen, migration is often a costly and time-consuming process. This paper presents Multi-Box, a lightweight container technology that facilitates flexible vendor-independent migration. Our framework allows its users to deploy and migrate almost any application in its normal state with minimal computational and network resource overheads. We show that the performance overhead of deploying within a lightweight container is 4.90 % of the resources available to an average VM and downtime during a migration is less than the time needed to scale a server using provider-centric tools.

Keywords: Cloud computing · Multi-cloud systems · Containers · Workload migration

1 Introduction

The vision behind cloud computing is about liberating applications from the underlying resources, and allowing them to flexibly adapt according to their demand in order to optimise their operation. The current reality of cloud computing, however, is that such idealistic freedom does not exist. Cloud service providers (CSPs) do not support cross-provider workload management or migration. Some standardisation efforts subsist[1] but are yet largely disregarded by CSPs (for obvious commercial reasons) and by developers alike [1]. In face of such well-documented vendor-lockin (cf. [2,3]), workload migration becomes a challenging, manual and bespoke effort to take into account the CSPs' divergent application programming interfaces (APIs), the multitude of heterogeneous services, and disparate pricing schemes.

Additionally, current workload migration approaches are inattentive to network overheads which makes them unsuitable for deployments over long-latency networks and, potentially, rather costly. This limits many application deployments both geographically and dynamically, posing serious restrictions over the

---

[1] http://www.occi-wg.org/.

© Springer International Publishing Switzerland 2015
R. Horne (Ed.): EGC 2015, CCIS 514, pp. 79–90, 2015.
DOI: 10.1007/978-3-319-25043-4_8

ability of an application to adapt to its demand. This is unsatisfactory at a time
when application lifespans are becoming more volatile in light of agile development cycles of different resource usage profiles, and the use of social media that
can cause sudden and dramatic unexpected demand fluctuations and geographical spread.

In this paper, we define workload fluidity as the capability to migrate one
or more applications from one CSP to another at short notice with little or no
human intervention. Our key contribution is a method of achieving workload
fluidity by utilising extremely lightweight containers based on a relatively new
addition to the Linux kernel, known as control groups (cgroups)[2].

We use the term 'container' to refer to a lightweight isolated environment
wherein applications can be deployed, whilst staying decoupled from the host.
Such execution environment is similar to a virtual machine (VM) but without a complete operating system (OS). Crucially, we focus on a highly flexible
decoupling that supports an extremely low performance overhead, and reduces
migration time and complexity to an absolute minimum.

The contributions of our MultiBox framework we present here are as follows:

1. A means of deploying both stateful and stateless applications (in their normal
   condition) to an environment decoupled from the host and other applications
   running inside it;
2. Our containers do not require the cooperation of CSPs as long as they provide
   Linux VMs, a novel contribution;
3. Reducing the impact of migrating an application when compared to other
   means including CSP-centric tools; and
4. Accommodating a wider range of applications with less complexity and performance overhead than other similar approaches.

These contributions are aimed at reducing development time spent on workload management, and at expanding a business's choice of CSPs by negating
the need for CSP cooperation. They also support workload incubation in a local
execution environment and cost-effective deployment and migration where connectivity is limited and/or costly.

The remainder of the paper is organised as follows: Sect. 2 outlines related
work. Section 3 describes the MultiBox requirements and design. Section 4 details
the technical implementation. Section 5 evaluates workload migration using
MultiBox through use cases on two contrasting CSPs. Section 6 concludes and
highlight future directions.

2   Related Work

Existing work on cloud workload management falls into two categories: *inside-
out* and *outside-in*. Inside-out approaches focus on altering the application code
to manage dependencies and enable cross-compatibility. This is highly complex

---

[2] https://www.kernel.org/doc/Documentation/cgroups/cgroups.txt.

as it requires the developers to be aware of the needs of the application before it is deployed and to alter the programming process to meet the needs of the toolkit being used [4–6]. Outside-in approaches, on the other hand, focus on managing the cloud infrastructure that supports given applications so that the same business objectives can be achieved via cloud brokerage. This generally limits an environment to one stateless application. The role of the cloud broker can be highly complex as it needs to be aware of the application, the CSPs involved and the interfaces to connect to each CSP. It may also include a decision-making engine supporting policies, negotiation and enforcement [7–9].

What is considered 'traditional' cloud deployment management is done through VMs, a heavyweight task requiring substantial computational resources to run a complete guest OS as well as high bandwidth for migrating VMs. Current literature on workload migration deals in one way or another with the substantial overhead of shifting VM images either within (cf. [10,11]) or between datacenters (cf. [12,13]). However, all previous work avoids the real issue of inter-cloud migration by assuming a common API either of a single CSP (the former examples) or a federation of clouds (the latter).

Another approach is to avoid shifting heavy VMs and instead attempt to recreate deployments through Configuration Management Tools (CMTs). CMTs, such as Chef[3] and Ansible[4], allow for the definition of an infrastructure in the form of code. Apart from the fact that they are catered towards VM-based appliances not containers, CMTs are transitional and non-deterministic: They assume a certain initial state, usually a blank OS, then alter this state rather than defining it. This more often than expected leads to undesirable results in different environments (CSPs, OSs) [14].

To our knowledge, no other work has tackled workload migration as represented by containers as a resource-efficient and CSP-independent solution.

Previous efforts, however, have differed on defining a container. Some have a limited view and only encapsulate a certain application such as a web service [15,16] as a monolithic appliance. The Elastic Application Container (EAC) [17] has a more generic definition that includes any application, but only allows for one instance per container. The EAC architecture prioritises container scalability and low overhead but not portability: EACs are managed by an Elastic Application Server which is analogous to a hypervisor running in the host OS. In contrast, our containers run using the Linux native cgroups, further reducing management overhead and supporting portability to any Linux host.

Our definition of a container agrees with those of technologies such as Docker[5], Linux-VServer[6] and OpenVZ[7]: a highly flexible abstraction of OS capabilities to enable applications to run in a virtual environment with low performance overhead, and at low migration time and complexity. Many of the

---

[3] http://www.chef.io/.

[4] http://www.ansible.com/.

[5] http://www.docker.com/.

[6] http://linux-vserver.org/.

[7] http://openvz.org/.

mentioned solutions, however, are designed to cater for immutable appliances. They do not include system services and daemons necessary for running stateful applications or operating multiple thereof.

3 MultiBox Design

We opt for a minimalist container-driven design to offer the user flexibility, low performance overhead and the capability to migrate applications quickly. We draw a parallel between the exokernel[8] approach to OS kernels and our approach to containers in that we "give as much safe, efficient control over system resources as possible" [18]. To do this, we design a lightweight implementation that makes heavy use of Linux control groups, an existing feature in modern Linux kernels.

3.1 Requirements

Our container implementation must be lightweight so that it does not occupy noticeable resources on the VM. This is important for two reasons. First, resources occupied on the VM are unavailable to the container. A sizeable implementation could mean that a tradeoff emerges between cost savings in migratability and cost savings in VM size. Second, a smaller implementation is more easily portable. As our key aim is portability, this can be partially achieved by reducing the number of framework files copied and compiled on each VM.

In addition to its weight, the flexibility offered to the developer is significant. A flexible framework allows developers to deploy their applications without modifications. Typically an application may require system resources including users, devices and storage. All of these must be visible through the container abstraction layer.

Finally, we consider compatibility. CSPs offer heterogeneous operating system templates. There may be variance in the choice of offered distributions, versions, architectures and packages. To facilitate mutli-cloud deployments, we must ensure compatibility with as many CSPs as possible by connecting to the commonalities.

3.2 Design Choices

By utilising key features present within the OS's kernel already, there is little duplication of code, little to install or ensure compatibility with above the kernel and little software to transport from one server to another during migration. We prioritise utilising kernel support and adopt a lightweight approach where this is not possible. We rely on a one-to-one relationship between hosts and containers to reduce the number of required costly features and restrictions. For example,

---

[8] Exokernel is an operating system kernel that forces as few abstractions as possible onto developers.

we do not superimpose a virtualised file system (such as Ploop[9] or AUFS[10], which can offer additional resource management tools) on to that of the host. Additionally, we deploy our management toolkit as a single init script with a number of connected system 'services'. The toolkit is thus simple to use, simple to call automatically and enables rapid installation on any Linux server.

We also rely on delta synchronisation for deployment and thus offer key system devices and file system read-write access where other container technologies, that rely on pre-specified metadata for deployment, do not. Specialised packages are not needed, which enables compatibility with a wider range of applications, including stateful applications, and enables application developers to deploy their application as they would normally.

We recognise that migration is necessary when moving any stateful application and aim to automate the process and reduce the migration time as much as possible. Migrating an application manually from one server to another involves installing an OS, adding common libraries, application dependencies and the application itself and finally installing any data upon which the application relies. However, by separating the running environment from the host's OS, this process can be automated. Thus, the handover time from one server to another is reduced and no manual intervention is needed.

3.3 System Components

A MultiBox container is a versatile execution environment supporting various processes, which are unaware of the remainder of the system. By using cgroups, a kernel module that provides support for the separation of processes into namespaces, a container is created as a namespace within the host to isolate its own processes, system and network devices, and file system (as depicted in Fig. 1). The functionality given to a container constitutes a smaller subset of an OS than that of other container managers to ensure that operation and migration overheads are minimised. It also includes the facilities for services, daemons, syslog, cron and running multiple applications. It makes use of the host's file system to minimise complexity, maximise performance and support stateful applications (Fig. 1).

MultiBox containers are managed by a Container Manager that creates the namespace, routes network traffic to the host and its containers, and allocates resources to the container to support running applications. It also facilitates user interaction with the namespace. The Container Manager manages the few dependencies that are required outside the container. These include certain OS networking capabilities and a compiler.

A repository is maintained from which subsequent deployments will copy an OS template. Deltas, including the application and its dependencies, are then synchronised from a separate location in a second pass. The duration of this second pass depends partly on the type of application that is running within the

---

[9] http://openvz.org/Ploop.

[10] http://aufs.sourceforge.net/aufs.html.

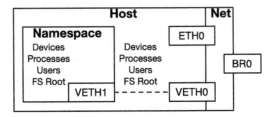

Fig. 1. The MultiBox architecture

container, though it is expected to be small relative to the data copied in the first pass. It also depends on the connection between the two VMs. In general, we expect that the first pass involves more data transferred at a higher speed than the second pass. This accounts for a potentially greater latency and lower bandwidth between the two servers at this stage, enabling a local or development server to synchronise with a production server elsewhere.

4   Implementation

The implementation consists of two key elements: kernel support for cgroups and the container manager. We now describe how these elements are implemented.

4.1   Kernel Support for Control Groups

Control groups allow for a system's resources to be divided into namespaces. They were designed to segregate concerns within a large system that, for example, may operate as a file server and a web server. These namespaces can then be treated as separate systems. This works via a kernel module, written in the C language, that isolates processes into groups. Allocated or unallocated resources, including memory, disk and network, can be assigned to a portion of the system. Devices can also be presented to the namespace. This portion of the system has a directory within the main system that it uses as its root, similar to a chroot environment. The capability to assign resources as well as processes to a namespace makes control groups suitable for containers.

Kernel support is needed to run control groups within a VM. The lightweight cgroups package provides this functionality that can be compiled into a standard 3.x kernel. To facilitate easy deployments, we compiled Kernel 3.14.22 with support for control groups. We also included support for paravirtualised environments to enable compatibility with a larger number of CSPs. The built kernel was compiled into an RPM package to enable easy installation on RedHat Linux systems such as those running RHEL, CentOS and Scientific Linux. We chose this type of package to support a wide range of OSs easily, though other packages could also be created to support other distributions.

4.2   Container Manager

The container manager utilises cgroups to prepare a VM to run a container and to migrate a container from a separate VM. The container manager was implemented as an init script supporting the five following commands.

The **prepare** command runs on a fresh VM to download and install the pre-built kernel, toolkit and other packages necessary to support containers from a central repository. It also makes configuration changes to run the new kernel, support the OS-level IP forwarding needed to forward connections from the VM to the container and creates the base directory for the container.

The **create** command initiates a fresh container the first time that containers are implemented in an environment. It downloads and extracts a blank OS template file into the container's root directory from a remote repository.

When a container is ready to be run, **boot** is invoked. It also runs as part of the VM's subsequent start-up sequences. It begins by detaching any existing containers running on the VM by analysing the running processes and active devices on the VM. It then creates a new container within a background process on the VM, utilising the OS files located in the container's root directory. A virtual Ethernet and network bridge are created to support network communication between the container and the Internet. We assume that the VM has one IP address allocated to it and nothing else running on it. Thus, we move SSH on the VM to port 65535 and forward traffic on all other ports to the container. Then, a virtual Ethernet device is moved to the container's namespace and traffic is routed through it. Finally, a subset of the standard OS initialisation commands are run within the container to start application-dependent services.

sync creates a new SSH key pair if one does not exist on the VM. It uploads the public key to the old VM and runs **resync** for the first time. This is intended to be run when a migration is requested. Finally, the **resync** command synchronises the container's root directory from one host to another. It does this by downloading deltas from the old VM using the **rsync** utility present in Linux.

4.3   Overall Workflow

The container manager was integrated with a backend PHP program to make API calls to CSPs. The overall process is as depicted in Fig. 2. We have adopted a final offline synchronisation pass as live migration techniques used in deployments such as [19] would not have improved efficiency where an IP change is necessary. Each step in the workflow diagram is performed once although file deltas could be copied several times where the ratio of network throughput to file changes is low.

We now examine each step in detail.

Allocation: A new VM is created at a CSP. This is performed by the backend application using calls to the CSP's API. Most CSPs expose powerful APIs, many of which can also be used to collect data about the CSP's offerings. As such, decisions could be made in real time concerning which CSP to deploy to, based on usage data already collected and/or user preferences.

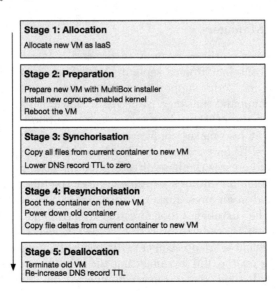

Fig. 2. The MultiBox workflow

Preparation: Preparing a new VM with the MultiBox installer consists of a single call to the MultiBox program. This command is also run by the backend application. The MultiBox program downloads and installs system dependencies, including the cgroups-enabled kernel. It also makes changes to the operating system to support IP forwarding.

Synchronisation: Files are copied using the `rsync` Linux utility, which is based on the SSH protocol. The TTL on the DNS record is lowered by the PHP application via a call to the DNS provider's API. A TTL of zero ensures that the record is not cached, increasing the overhead on the DNS service but ensuring the fastest transition.

Resynchronisation: The boot process on the new container depends on the operating system to be booted. For example, on Red Hat Linux, the `chkconfig` utility provides a list of services to be started at runtime. This is used to generate a list of commands for execution. These commands are run in a shell in the container's namespace. Commands are also run on the new VM, outside the container to forward traffic to and from the container. The container on the old VM is shut down via a Shell command.

Deallocation: The old VM is terminated via a call to the CSP's API and the DNS record is re-increased via a call to the DNS provider's API.

5   Evaluation

We confirm the efficacy of our framework in migrating stateful and stateless applications between clouds by successfully migrating a running Minecraft game server and an Apache web server from Softlayer to Vultr. In the case of the stateful application, a client connected to the game server was able to reconnect within a few seconds without changes to the connection settings or the game's state. In the case of the stateless application, a client browsing the hosted website did not notice any interruption.

The result of only migrating *moving parts*, i.e. application-specific logic, data and dependencies, offers improvements over full VM migration and recipe-based deployment. In full VM migration, the whole OS and shared libraries are moved. Such migration process moves *gigabytes* of data across the network and thus cannot be achieved without noticeable interruption (and cost). By contrast, the moving parts generally account for *megabytes* of data. In recipe-based deployment, there is no support for the deployment and migration of stateful applications and developer time is under greater demand with regard to recipe and repository creation and maintenance.

We continue to evaluate the efficacy of our framework by analysing two metrics. First, we compare the migration-related delay and downtime with a stateful and a stateless application by scaling the existing VM using provider-centric tools. Second, we measure the performance penalty of deploying and running an application within our framework relative to deploying directly to the VM.

5.1   Deployment Overhead

To measure the performance impact of running our framework, we deployed an instance on the Softlayer cloud[11]. We first ran the Geekbench Linux benchmarking utility to obtain a score for the memory and CPU performance in 32-bit mode. We then created a container and ran the same test within the container.

The Geekbench benchmarking utility produces scores against a 2500 baseline score; the higher the score the better the performance. Geekbench yielded a multi-threaded score of 7709 outside the container and 7331 inside the container. Whereas both scores are acceptable for a VM of 4 CPU cores and 8 GB memory, there is a reduction in performance of 4.90 % inside the container. As the container's overhead is fixed, this overhead is expected to form a larger percentage of available resources on a small VM and a smaller percentage on a larger VM.

5.2   Migration Time

To accurately measure the migration delay and downtime, we install a stateless web server in one container and a stateful client-server game, Minecraft, in another. We then construct a simulator in PHP to initialise the migration process using our framework and to record the time at different points. Both the stateful and stateless servers are accessible via a DNS "address" record with its TTL set to zero. The DNS server is external.

The simulator initially prompts the user for the VM's current IP address, and the destination CSP of choice from Softlayer and Vultr. Softlayer, IBM's

---

[11] We ran this test on Softlayer only as resources on the Vultr cloud are subject to the 'noisy neighbours' phenomenon.

public cloud offering, represents larger clouds with greater elasticity, complexity and cost, while Vultr represents smaller clouds at the other end of the respective spectrums. Each CSP has a different delay and downtime profile.

The simulator then creates a new VM with the chosen CSP, connects to the new VM and runs `prepare` and `sync`. Then, it connects to the DNS server to update the corresponding record and runs `resync`. Timestamps are taken at the beginning, after the VM creation, after running `sync` and upon completion. Thus, we obtain three time durations: the time to create the VM at the CSP; the time to prepare, sync and boot the container; and the final switchover time.

We also continuously connect to the server running within each container. For the stateless web server, this is achieved by periodically fetching a web page. For the stateful game, it is achieved by running an instance of the game's client elsewhere. In both cases, the server is contacted via the DNS name. We record the downtime, i.e. the time during which no server is available at that address.

We compare these times with the times taken to scale the server at the current CSP. This is acquired by starting a timer when an upgrade process is initialised using the CSP's own toolkit for greater CPU, memory and disk resources. The time taken after the request is created but before the server is shutdown is recorded. Additionally, the time taken for the server to be booted with the new resource set is recorded.

Figure 2 shows a comparison between these metrics after 500 s. Note that in each case, the delay before taking a server offline was greater with our migration framework but that period during which service was unavailable was greater with the CSP-provided tools. This result is quite significant as the delay can often be predicted and planned to reduce the impact on business operation.

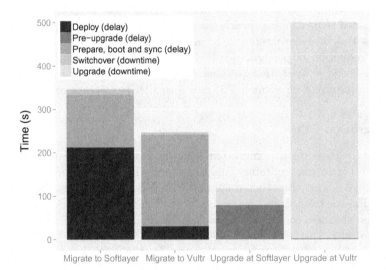

Fig. 3. Plot of migration and upgrade-related delays at two CSPs

Furthermore, errors during the migration process can be easily recovered from via re-deployment, whereas errors during the upgrade process are more complex to recover from.

5.3   Human Costs and Portability

The cost of deploying and re-deploying (i.e. migrating) MultiBox containers on the developer is very low. The process is deterministic as dependencies are explicitly defined and natively provisioned. This is in comparison to CMTs where the desired execution environment is surprisingly not guaranteed across CSPs and OSs [14].

MultiBox supports portability of containers by design. The MultiBox implementation (kernel and command line tools) are OS agnostic, enabling easy deployment to any Linux-based host. This is significant as CSPs offers different sets of Linux distributions. Such Linux-native support sets MultiBox apart in its support for container migration from all other similar efforts (Fig. 3).

6   Conclusion

This paper presented MultiBox, a means of creating and migrating containers. MultiBox containers are isolated form the rest of the host OS through the use of Linux cgroups to create namespaces. MultiBox containers can support multiple stateful processes as well as other OS-level services and file system.

The Linux-native aspect of MultiBox containers offer great advantages: they are transferable to any CSP infrastructure that supports any Linux variant. This means that CSP cooperation is *not* required, which is a groundbreaking advancement in the area of cross-cloud computing. Furthermore, MultiBox containers are lightweight by design and migrating them is significantly more resource efficient than other cloud workload migration approaches.

Also presented in the paper is a preliminary evaluation of MultiBox management and migration overheads. More experiments using larger cloud deployments and a thorough analysis of the different overheads is planned as future work.

References

1. Johnston, S.: Simple workload & application portability (swap). In: The 1st International Workshop on CrossCloud Computing (CrossCloud), pp. 37–42 (2014)
2. Nguyen, D.K., Taher, Y., Papazoglou, M., van den Heuvel, W.: Service-based application development on the cloud: state-of-the-art and shortcoming analysis. In: International Conference on Cloud Computing and Services Science (CLOSER 2012) (2012)
3. Petcu, D., Macariu, G., Panica, S., Crăciun, C.: Portable cloud applications-from theory to practice. Future Gener. Comput. Syst. **29**(6), 1417–1430 (2013)
4. Vadhiyar, S.S., Dongarra, J.J.: SRS: a framework for developing malleable and migrateable parallel applications for distributed systems. Parallel Process. Lett. **13**, 291–312 (2003)

5. Guillén, J., Miranda, J., Murillo, J.M., Canal, C.: A service-oriented framework for developing cross cloud migratable software. J. Syst. Softw. **86**(9), 2294–2308 (2013)
6. Miranda, J., Guillén, J., Murillo, J.M., Canal, C.: Enough about standardization, let's build cloud applications. In: Proceedings of the ACM WICSA/ECSA 2012 Companion Volume, pp. 74–77 (2012)
7. Pawluk, P., Simmons, B., Smit, M., Litoiu, M., Mankovski, S.: Introducing STRATOS: a cloud broker service. In: International Conference on Cloud Computing (IEEE CLOUD), pp. 891–898 (2012)
8. Nair, S., Porwal, S., Dimitrakos, T., Ferrer, A., Tordsson, J., Sharif, T., Sheridan, C., Rajarajan, M., Khan, A.: Towards secure cloud bursting, brokerage and aggregation. In: European Conference on Web Services (IEEE ECOWS), pp. 189–196 (2010)
9. Samreen, F., Blair, G.S., Rowe, M.: Adaptive decision making in multi-cloud management. In: The 2nd International Workshop on CrossCloud Computing (CrossCloud), CCB 2014, pp. 4:1–4:6. ACM (2014)
10. Hirofuchi, T., Nakada, H., Itoh, S., Sekiguchi, S.: Enabling instantaneous relocation of virtual machines with a lightweight VMM extension. In: International Conference on Cluster, Cloud and Grid Computing (IEEE/ACM CCGrid), pp. 73–83 (2010)
11. Han, R., Guo, L., Ghanem, M., Guo, Y.: Lightweight resource scaling for cloud applications. In: International Symposium on Cluster, Cloud and Grid Computing (IEEE/ACM CCGrid), pp. 644–651 (2012)
12. Celesti, A., Tusa, F., Villari, M., Puliafito, A.: Improving virtual machine migration in federated cloud environments. In: International Conference on Evolving Internet (INTERNET), pp. 61–67 (2010)
13. Cerroni, W.: Multiple virtual machine live migration in federated cloud systems. In: The 1st International Workshop on CrossCloud Computing (CrossCloud), pp. 25–30 (2014)
14. Zhu, L., Xu, D., Xu, X.S., Tran, A.B., Weber, I., Bass, L.: Challenges in practicing high frequency releases in cloud environments. In: International Workshop on Release Engineering, Mountain View, USA, pp. 21–24 (2014)
15. Mohamed, M., Yangui, S., Moalla, S., Tata, S.: Web service micro-container for service-based applications in cloud environments. In: International Workshops on Enabling Technologies: Infrastructure for Collaborative Enterprises (IEEE WET-ICE), pp. 61–66 (2011)
16. Yangui, S., Mohamed, M., Tata, S., Moalla, S.: Scalable service containers. In: International Conference on Cloud Computing Technology and Science (IEEE CloudCom), pp. 348–356 (2011)
17. He, S., Guo, L., Guo, Y., Wu, C., Ghanem, M., Han, R.: Elastic application container: a lightweight approach for cloud resource provisioning. In: International Conference on Advanced Information Networking and Applications (AINA), pp. 15–22 (2012)
18. Engler, D.R.: The exokernel operating system architecture. Ph.D. thesis, Massachusetts Institute of Technology (1998)
19. Clark, C., Fraser, K., Hand, S., Hansen, J.G., Jul, E., Limpach, C., Pratt, I., Warfield, A.: Live migration of virtual machines. In: Proceedings of the 2nd Conference on Symposium on Networked Systems Design & Implementation, vol. 2, pp. 273–286. USENIX Association (2005)

Texture Recognition by Spatially Adaptive Classification

Anatoly Kornev[✉]

Kazakh-British Technical University, 59 Tole bi Str., 050000 Almaty, Kazakhstan
entapp@ro.ru

Abstract. The image preprocessing and the skeleton orientation method are applied to segment a texture image with structure-oriented patterns. The technique is incorporated with a spatially adaptive classification of geometric features. The algorithm is tested on a set of artificial images and X-ray tomography scan of titanium alloy. The results are presented and discussed.

Keywords: Texture recognition · Thresholding · Scale axis transform · kNN classification

1 Introduction

The detection of texture and edges is an important step for further object extraction and classification. In aerospace, power generation and biomedical industries there is a set of complex problems which has to be addressed by better description of visual features and improvement of the extraction procedure. For example, titanium alloys are widely used in many mission-critical and health-related products. The mechanical properties of these alloys, especially fatigue, are strongly dependent on formation of the microstructure during solidification process. In the samples reconstructed from X-ray tomography scans the internal micro-structures like the β-grains and α-lamellars, represent as edges with different thickness and orientation. Thus the micro-structure orientation provides an important information for crack analysis in the accident investigation.

The recent status in processing of images with texture is reflected in numerous reviews and monographs [1–8]. The references also cite medical, remote sensing, and other applications. Due to enormous amount of publications in the area a very brief overview of existing and prospective methods for the analysis of textures is presented.

The texture description and extraction may be roughly divided on a number of categories:

1. statistical;
2. structural included spectral analysis, filter banks, patterns, and fractals;
3. crystallographic; and
4. a combination of above methods.

© Springer International Publishing Switzerland 2015
R. Horne (Ed.): EGC 2015, CCIS 514, pp. 91–100, 2015.
DOI: 10.1007/978-3-319-25043-4_9

The statistical approach characterizes a texture by the statistical moments. Additionally, texture metrics may contain spatial information. The spatial data considered is the relative position of pairs of pixels, defined with distance and orientation that describe the location of the second pixel with respect to the first. Among the popular methods are a grey level co-occurrence matrix and a histogram features analysis. The statistical methods will give an average description of texture and will certainly not provide enough possibility of reconstruction [5, 7].

For periodic and quasi-periodic textures such as textiles and a like, it is natural to consider the use of structural (transform-based) and spectral methods. Oriented Gabor and difference of Gaussian (DOG) filters, and Laws texture energy measures illustrate the use of specialized image filters for texture analysis. The Fourier and wavelets transforms of original image allow to generate a set of new features for texture description. The statistical analysis of frequency components and magnitude of transform data may lead to a reduced set of features. Structural and spectral methods possess an extreme ability to localize structures in time and frequency domain, but a penalty of greater computational complexity. More recent developments include fractal-based measures, Markov random fields, and Local Binary Patterns (LBP) techniques [5, 9].

Despite certain achievements, especially for parts of image with different colors, there is a lack of methods which are dealing with structure-oriented patterns. Moreover, texture information is also present in form of volumetric data and can be quantified by estimating of local structure orientation. In [10] it was proposed a fast method to estimate local orientations from the covariance matrix of the image gradient. The authors [11] created a new 3D filter, called the CHG (Complementary of HourGlass) and the corresponding directional filter bank (DFB) to retrieve the orientation and the boundaries of lamellar colonies in $(\alpha+\beta)$ titanium alloys. The covariance matrix and the filtering techniques rely on the image resolution and the size of neighbourhood around every studied pixel or voxel: this one must contain a certain amount of pixels for the algorithm precision.

An alternative approach is evolved in materials science [3, 8]. The texture is determined as a distribution of crystallographic orientations of a polycrystalline sample. For no texture case these orientations are fully random in a sample. The texture degree depends on the percentage of crystals having the preferred orientation. The most widely used method of texture detection is a X-ray diffraction, followed by the electron backscatter diffraction (EBSD) in the scanning electron microscope.

Historically, the crystallographic texture is described by the pole figure, based on the stereographic projection and the orientation distribution function (ODF), positioned on the three Euler angles of rotation required to orientate a unit cell with a reference coordinate system. Measurements of pole figures by means of X-ray diffraction started in the 1940s. The prevalent approach to texture research before the 1980s was the use of X-rays to probe the average texture of a specimen. Neutron diffraction offers some advantages, which are mainly attributed to the much lower absorption of neutrons. The typical cases for pole figures with a random and a dominant textures are shown in Fig. 1.

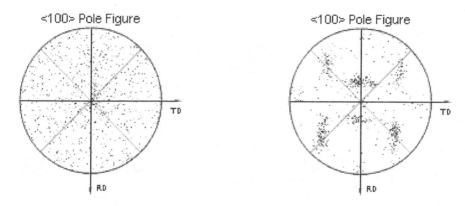

Fig. 1. Pole figure showing a random texture (left) and a preferred texture (right). The image is a courtesy of European Aluminium Association.

A specified crystallographic axis (or pole) from each of a representative number of crystallites is plotted in a stereographic projection, along with directions stored in the material's processing history. These directions are commonly referred to as the rolling direction RD and the transverse direction TD, as shown in the Fig. 1. Both X-ray diffraction and EBSD may collect pole figures by using integral transform.

The 3D representation of crystallographic texture is given by the orientation distribution function (ODF) which can be achieved through estimation of a set of pole figures or diffraction spectra. It describes the orientations in 3D space of thousands or millions of individual grains. The ODFs cannot be directly measured by means of diffraction techniques. Instead, they need to be calculated from the pole figure information, typically from a number of different pole figures obtained from a given sample. The ODF is defined as a probability density function of orientations $g = \phi_1, \Phi, \phi_2$ in the form of the Euler angles ϕ_1, Φ, and ϕ_2 [3]

$$\frac{dV}{V} = f(g)dg, \quad \text{and} \quad \oint f(g)dg = 1, \tag{1}$$

where $dg = \frac{1}{8\pi^2} sin\Phi \, d\phi_1 \, d\phi_2$, V is the sample volume and dV is the volume of all crystallites with the orientation g in the angular element dg. The projection of the 3-D orientation distribution onto a 2-D plane results in a loss of information. Therefore, the 3-D orientation distribution cannot be derived from a pole figure without some uncertainty. A pole figure $P_h(y)$ corresponds to a region in the 3-D ODF $f(g)$ that contains all possible rotations with angle γ around the direction $y = \alpha, \beta$ and $dy = sin\alpha \, d\alpha \, d\beta$

$$P_h(y) = \frac{1}{2\pi} \int_{\gamma=0}^{2\pi} f(g)d\gamma, \tag{2}$$

A typical ODF for hot-rolled aluminum at the different sections of angle ϕ_2 is shown in Fig. 2.

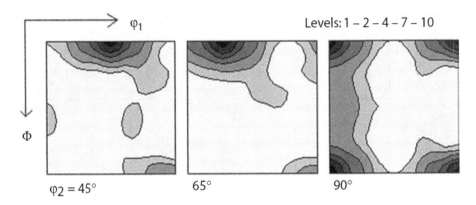

Fig. 2. ODF of hot-rolled aluminum for $\phi_2 = 45°, 65°, 90°$ sections [3].

The major drawback of crystallographic methods is a processing in transformed geometry and coordinate system, so that it will be difficult to compare with data from Cartesian coordinates.

The combined approach tries to gain advantages of all above techniques. Namely, it incorporate geometrical structures with statistical description [12]. In many applications, the essential shape information of a structure is obtained by representing it with its skeleton made of the medial lines along the main components of the structure. Thinning algorithms produce the skeleton by using criteria that search for the medial lines. The medial axis transform (MAT) determines the medial line by computing the distance d from each interior pixel of a binary structure to each boundary pixel. Since the concept of roughness is often associated with the size of the grain in the object, texture measures that rely on spatial information may be valuable [13].

The goal of this paper is to present a simple and complete model for texture detection and extraction for specific X-ray images. The proposed technique has several aspects that are important to emphasize.

1. The preprocessing by histogram equalization and by thresholding.
2. The extraction of the structural features by the scale axis transform and the formulation of the classification procedure.

2   Preprocessing

The real images contain the noise from a variety of sources. Thus we recommend some contrast and brightness enhancements together with linear and non-linear filtering if it is required [7].

The histogram equalization is often used for X-ray images because they have a small signal-to-noise ratio. To transfer an image to the binary format, the histogram thresholding is applied.

The Otsu method [14] is utilized to convert the original image to the corresponding binary one.

1. Consider an initial threshold T, e.g. mean value of all pixels in the image.
2. Split the histogram of the image into two sets: background and foreground or object parts.

$$background = I(i,j) \leq T, \tag{3}$$

$$foreground = I(i,j) > T, \tag{4}$$

where i and j are a pixel coordinates and I is an intensity of the image.
3. Calculate the average of each set

$$a_1 = I(i,j) \leq T/N_1, \tag{5}$$

$$a_2 = I(i,j) > T/N_2, \tag{6}$$

where N_1, N_2 are a numbers of pixels in each set.
4. Create a new threshold as an average of both sets

$$T = (a_1 + a_2)/2. \tag{7}$$

5. Iterate from step two to step four by using an updated threshold value T.

3   Texture Recognition

The texture extraction algorithm may be defined as follows.

1. Apply scale axis transform to the binary image. The scale axis transform uses a scaling of medial balls to identify significant features of the object shape. The s-scale axis transform of a shape S is determined by the following construction: (i) calculate the medial axis of S yielding the union of medial balls, (ii) increase the radius of each medial ball by the factor $s \geq 1$, (iii) recalculate the medial axis of the scaled union of balls, and (iv) decrease the new medial balls by the inverse factor $1/s$. The final set of balls is the $s-$scale axis transform of shape S and the ball centers define the corresponding $s-$scale axis. For factor $s = 1$ the scale axis transform is identical to the medial axis transform, and larger values of s lead to higher levels of simplification. The pruning step is based on a topology-preserving version of the angle filtration [15]. The example of scale axis filtration on complex shape for different object angles is shown in Fig. 3.
2. Calculate a skeleton orientation in each of the directions $0 < \theta < 350°$ incremented by $\Delta\theta = 10°$. In Fig. 4 it is presented for $\Delta\theta = 30°$.
3. Apply a smoothing procedure for pixels along the given skeleton.
4. Introduce a palette with 18 colors: each color represents a certain orientation with the increment of 10 degree.
5. Mark pixels along the selected skeleton by appropriate color from a palette according to its orientation.

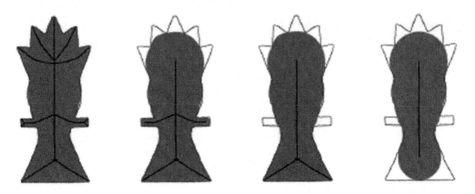

Fig. 3. The discrete scale axis representations based on pruning by object angle [15].

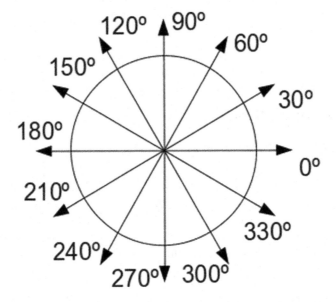

Fig. 4. The line orientations for $\Delta\theta = 30°$, 12 directions in the case.

3.1 kNN Classification

The pixels, which do not belong to the skeleton, are classified by the k nearest neighbours (kNN) method [5]. The kNN uses an assumption that samples of a dataset with similar properties will exist in close proximity. To classify an unlabeled sample, the k nearest samples are located and the most frequent class label is assigned to the unlabeled sample. The method is performed with Euclidean distance as the similarity measure, and a fixed number of nearest neighbours are considered for majority voting.

We run a number of nearest neighbors using the values $k = 1, 3, ..., 11$ on the testing images. The optimal obtained k is then used to perform the calculations.

4   Results and Discussion

The proposed algorithm is tested on the artificial sample as shown in Fig. 5. The image parts with seven different texture orientations are combined to a single image. The angle resolution for the method is $\Delta\theta = 10°$. It is clear that the proposed technique is able to handle a different texture orientation properly see Fig. 6. Meanwhile, it can be seen that there are small distortions in the

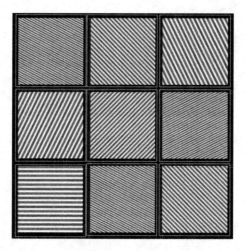

Fig. 5. The original image with parts of the different texture orientation.

Fig. 6. The result of processing: each color in the palette corresponds to a certain orientation (Color figure online).

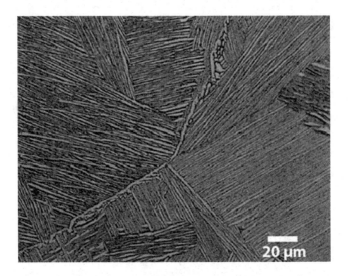

Fig. 7. The micro-structures in a X-ray scan of titanium alloy. The image is a courtesy of TiSonix Inc., USA

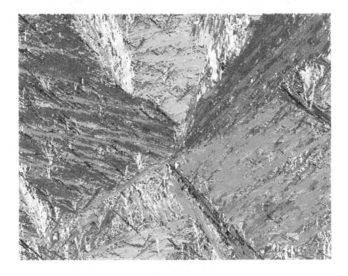

Fig. 8. The texture extraction from original X-ray image of titanium alloy.

calculations of the angle due to the precision of the method. Next, the model is applied to the experimental image which presents a X-ray tomography scan of the lamellar titanium alloy, see Fig. 7. The texture extraction by using the proposed method is illustrated in Fig. 8. Again, the color palette below the image represents a certain texture orientation with the angle step of 10 degree. In most parts of the image the algorithm handles the structure orientation correctly. The results of processing will help to estimate the grain structural features and to select the regions of potential crack initiation and propagation.

5   Conclusions

The texture detection model has been introduced as a recognition task for oriented structures in titanium alloys. The digital scale axis transform combined with kNN classification shows a good accuracy and a considerable reliability. The proposed approach can be easily, without any restrictions, extended to 3D and may be used in a common framework to analyze the objects with texture. Still, there are several issues which we intend to study in the future work. Namely, the considerable noise has to be suppressed. And, the interconnection zones between continuous texture areas might require a proper integration with edge detection routines.

Acknowledgements. The author would like to thank colleagues for many stimulating discussions, and to anonymous reviewers for helpful comments on the original version of the manuscript.

References

1. Petrou, M., Sevilla, P.G.: Image Processing Dealing with Texture. Wiley, New York (2006)
2. Tou, J.Y., Tay, Y.H., Lau, P.Y.: Recent trends in texture classification: a review. In: Symposium Progress in Information & Communication Technology, pp. 63–68 (2009)
3. Engler, O., Randle, V.: Introduction to Texture Analysis. Macrotexture, Microtexture, and Orientation Mapping. CRC Press, Boca Raton (2010)
4. Bankman, I.N.: Handbook of Medical Image Processing and Analysis, 2nd edn. Academic Press, San Diego (2009)
5. Davies, E.R.: Computer and Machine Vision: Theory, Algorithms, Practicalities. Academic Press, Oxford (2012)
6. Mirmehdi, M., Xie, X., Suri, J. (eds.): Handbook of Texture Analysis. Imperial College Press, London (2008)
7. Nixon, M., Aguado, A.: Feature Extraction and Image Processing. Newnes, Boston (2002)
8. Kocks, U.F., Tom, C.N., Wenk, H.-R.: Texture and Anisotropy, Preferred Orientations in Polycrystals and Their Effect on Materials Properties. Cambridge University Press, Cambridge (1998)
9. Pietikinen, M., Hadid, A., Zhao, G., Ahonen, T.: Computer Vision Using Local Binary Patterns. Springer, Heidelberg (2011)
10. Jeulin, D., Moreaud, M.: Segmentation of 2D and 3D textures from estimates of the local orientation. Image Anal. Stereol. **27**, 83–192 (2008)
11. Babout, L., Jopek, L., Janaszewski, M.: A new directional filter bank for 3D texture segmentation: application to lamellar microstructure in titanium alloys. In: MVA 2013 IAPR International Conference on Machine Vision Applications, Kyoto, Japan, pp. 419–422 (2013)
12. Chen, Y.Q., Nixon, M.S., Thomas, D.W.: Texture classification using statistical geometric features. Pattern Recog. **28**(4), 537–552 (1995)

13. Siddiqi, K., Pizer, S. (eds.): Medial Representations: Mathematics, Algorithms and Applications. Springer, Heidelberg (2008)
14. Otsu, A.: Threshold selection method from gray-level histogram. IEEE Trans. Syst. Man Cybern. **9**, 62 (1979)
15. Miklos, B., Giesen, J., Pauly, M.: Discrete scale axis representations for 3D geometry. ACM Trans. Graph. **29**, 4 (2010)

A Unifying Framework for Interactive Programming and Applications to Communicating Peer-to-Peer Systems

Alexandru Popa[1]([✉]), Iulia Teodora Banu-Demergian[4], Camelia Chira[3],
Florian Mircea Boian[2], and Gheorghe Stefanescu[4]

[1] School of Science and Technology, Nazarbayev University, Astana, Kazakhstan
`alexandru.popa@nu.edu.kz`
[2] Department of Computer Science, UBB, Cluj-Napoca, Romania
`florin@cs.ubbcluj.ro`
[3] Department of Computer Science, UTC, Cluj-Napoca, Romania
`camelia.chira@cs.utcluj.ro`
[4] Department of Computer Science, University of Bucharest, Bucharest, Romania
`th_iulia84@yahoo.com`, `gheorghe.stefanescu@fmi.unibuc.ro`

Abstract. We present a unifying framework for interactive programming built-up on top of rv-systems, a space-time invariant model for interactive computation which extends register machines with interactive capabilities. The framework provides a kernel coordination language parametrized by the programming language used for writing the code of the basic blocks. To illustrate the framework, we describe an implementation of an interactive communicating system where the nodes use Chord peer-to-peer communication protocol and their coordination is written in Agapia, a structured interactive programming language for rv-systems.

1 Interactive Programming, Coordination Languages

Interactive computation has a long tradition and there are many successful approaches to deal with the intricate aspects of this type of computation (see, for example, [1,4,10,19–21]. However, there is not yet an unifying foundation model or a simple and unifying implementation technology. Recently, we see a clear trend to separate the algorithmic part from the coordination part of the programming languages, by proposing simple coordination languages like REO [2] or Orc [14].

Stefanescu [17] proposes an unifying formalism for interactive systems to extend the classical imperative programming paradigm. The model is based on space-time duality and register machines. One of the key features of the model is the introduction of high-level temporal data structures. Actually, having high level temporal data on interaction interfaces is of crucial importance in getting a compositional model for interactive systems, a goal not always easy to achieve (recall the difficulties in getting a compositional semantics for data-flow networks). In a couple of papers [5–9,15,16], Dragoi and Stefanescu have developed

© Springer International Publishing Switzerland 2015
R. Horne (Ed.): EGC 2015, CCIS 514, pp. 101–112, 2015.
DOI: 10.1007/978-3-319-25043-4_10

structured programming techniques for rv-programs and a kernel programming languages for structured rv-systems, called AGAPIA v0.1.

In order to illustrate the expressiveness of the AGAPIA language, we present an implementation of Chord [18], a distributed lookup protocol that addresses one of the key problems of peer-to-peer applications, namely the efficient location of data items. Peer-to-peer systems are a hot topic of research and have connections to several areas such as: content delivery networks, cloud computing and data centers. For example, Kavalionak and Montresor propose a self-regulation mechanism that focuses on replica management in cloud-based, peer-assisted applications [12].

In [15] we consider a simpler case study: a protocol for the communication and termination detection in a cluster of computers, each having a dynamic set of running processes. Nevertheless, in this paper we present the implementation of a more complex protocol which is also frequently used.

The rest of the paper is organized as follows. In Sect. 2 we briefly introduce rv-systems and present the syntax of AGAPIA v0.1. Then, in Sect. 3 we give the details of the implementation. Finally, Sect. 4 is reserved for conclusions and future work.

2   Rv-systems and Agapia Programming

Rv-systems (interactive systems with registers and voices) [17] extend register machines with interactive capabilities. They provide an abstract and powerful space-time invariant model where high-level temporal data are used to structure the interaction interfaces of the processes. These temporal data types (including voices as a time-dual version of registers) are implemented on top of streams.

On top on rv-systems, structured programming techniques for rv-systems have been introduced with a particular emphasis on developing a structural spatial programming discipline [8]. The structured interaction between processes simplifies to a great deal the construction and the analysis of interactive programs [9]. Compared with other interaction calculi (e.g., π-calculus [13] or actor models [1]), structured rv-programming approach is based on a process name-free calculus. Adapting a slogan from classical structured programming, one may say that *"naming and calling processes by names is harmful."*

AGAPIA [8,15] (see Fig. 2) is a kernel high-level massively parallel, interactive programming language. The language is natural and expressive, for instance one can easily model the activity of a ring of processes in an open environment where processes may freely join or leave the ring. The language has simple denotational and operational semantics based on scenarios. (Scenarios are a two-dimensional extension of the running paths used in imperative programs, see Fig. 1.) It naturally supports process migration, structured interaction, and deployment of modules on heterogeneous machines.

In its first released version (v0.1), AGAPIA uses a "3-level" grammar for constructing rv-structured programs: first simple *while* programs are encapsulated in modules with simple spatial/temporal interfaces (*SST, STT*). Then, rv-programs are defined, applying rv-structured statements on top of modules. In

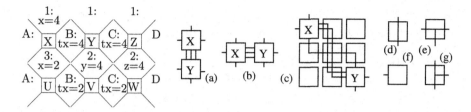

Fig. 1. A scenario and operations on scenarios

Interfaces

$SST ::= nil \mid sn \mid sb \mid (SST \cup SST)$
$\qquad \mid (SST, SST) \mid (SST)^*$

$ST ::= (SST) \mid (ST \cup ST)$
$\qquad \mid (ST; ST) \mid (ST;)^*$

$STT ::= nil \mid tn \mid tb \mid (STT \cup STT)$
$\qquad \mid (STT, STT) \mid (STT)^*$

$TT ::= (STT) \mid (TT \cup TT)$
$\qquad \mid (TT; TT) \mid (TT;)^*$

Expressions

$V ::= x : ST \mid x : TT \mid V(k)$
$\qquad \mid V.k \mid V.[k] \mid V@k \mid V@[k]$

$E ::= n \mid V \mid E + E \mid E * E \mid E - E \mid E/E$

$B ::= b \mid V \mid B\&\&B \mid B\|B \mid !B \mid E < E$

Programs

$W ::= nil \mid new\ x : SST \mid new\ x : STT$
$\qquad \mid x := E \mid if(B)\{W\}else\{W\}$
$\qquad \mid W; W \mid while(B)\{W\}$

$M ::= module\{listen\ x : STT\}\{read\ x : SST\}$
$\qquad \{W;\}\{speak\ x : STT\}\{write\ x : SST\}$

$P ::= nil \mid M \mid if(B)\{P\}else\{P\}$
$\qquad \mid P\%P \mid P\#P \mid P\$P$
$\qquad \mid while\_t(B)\{P\} \mid while\_s(B)\{P\}$
$\qquad \mid while\_st(B)\{P\}$

Fig. 2. The syntax of AGAPIA v0.1 programs

version AGAPIA v0.2 high-level structured interactive programs are obtained by allowing modules to encapsulate arbitrary AGAPIA programs. For this purpose, particular communication modules (*Scatter/Gather*) are introduced, acting as a bridge between simple (module) types and general (program) types. In *Scatter* and *Gather* modules either vertical or horizontal direction have empty interfaces, and their body contains only assignments.

It is known that functions or procedures do not increase the expressive power of flowchart programs. The same fact holds for rv-programs. Any high-level structured interactive program is equivalent to a program written in AGAPIA v0.1. However, the extension contributes to readable and modularized presentations of algorithms being also a promising lead in finding connections between rv-interactive programming and object oriented languages.

3   Case Study: Chord Protocol

In this section we present the implementation of the Chord protocol using AGAPIA programming language.

Overview of the Chord Protocol. The term "peer to peer" refers to distributed systems and applications with high degree of decentralization. Tasks and resources are shared among peers exchanging information directly between each other. Each node runs software equivalent in functionality, implementing both client and server operations.

Chord [18] is a distributed lookup protocol that addresses one of the key problems of peer-to-peer applications: efficient location of data items. Chord uses a consistent hashing function (such as SHA-1) to assign for each node (i.e. peer) and key (i.e. information) an m-bit identifier. Identifiers are ordered in an *identifier circle* modulo 2^m, providing support for the main operation: *map a given key onto a node*.

Key k is assigned to the first node whose identifier is equal to or follows (the identifier of) k in the identifier space. This node is denoted by *successor(k)*. Similarly the successor of a node n is denoted by *successor(n)*. An identifier circle with $m = 4$ is presented in Fig. 3(a). The circle contains the nodes: $0, 1, 7$ and 13. The successor of key 3 is 7, similarly key 16 is located in node 0 and key 1 in node 1. If node 4 joins the network (as in Fig. 3(b)) then the key 3 is assigned to 4, if the node 1 leaves the network the key 1 is also assigned to 4.

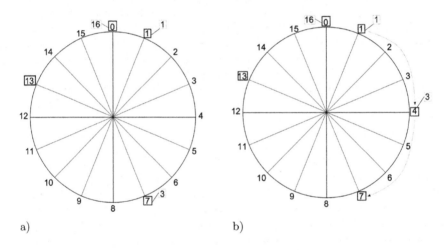

a)   b)

Fig. 3. Identifier circle for m = 4

When a node receives a look-up query for a certain key k, it may pass the query to its successor s. If node s is not the successor of k, the query is passed to s's successor, and so on. Hence, for a successful lookup, each node is required to maintain correct informations only about its direct successor. Yet, this approach may be inefficient as in some cases all nodes are to be traversed. In order to accelerate the computation of lookups, each node maintains small additional routing information about its closest neighbors. The routing table of a node, n, called *finger table*, contains $O(log\ N)$ nodes ids, where N is the maximum number of nodes in the system. The ith entry contains the identifier of the first node, s, satisfying $s = successor(n + 2^{i-1})$. The first finger is *successor(n)*. In the presentation of the algorithm the notation for s is *n.finger[i]*.

Figure 5 shows the pseudo-code of the lookup procedure that uses finger tables. If the searched key k falls between the node n and n's successor, n returns its successors. Otherwise, n passes the query to the node n' in the finger table, that is most closely preceding the searched key k. For example the node 1 is queried for the successor of key 12. The largest finger of 1, preceding 12 is 7, 1 passes the query to node 7. Since 12 is between 7 and its successor 13, the final result is 13.

The number of messages transfered in a lookup query is $O(logN)$.

```
n.stabilize()
    x = successor.get_predecessor();
    if (x in (n,successor))
        successor = x;
    successor.notify(n);

n.check_predecessor()
    if (failed(predecessor))
        predecessor = nil;

n.notify(n')
    if (predecessor is nil or n' in (predecessor,n))
        predecessor = n'

n.build_fingers(n')
    for i index in finger[]
        finger[i] = n'.find_successor(n+2^(i-1))

n.join(n')
    predecessor = nil;
    s = n'.find_successor(n);
    build_fingers(s);
    successor = s;
```

Fig. 4. Procedures for stabilization and node joins

Chord must ensure correct lookups in dynamic networks where nodes leave (fail) or join arbitrarily, by maintaining reachability of all nodes in the system. When a new node n joins the network, it asks another node n' to find its successor, yet the rest of the network is not aware of n. Newly joined nodes are detected as each node runs periodically a stabilization procedure. When a node n executes *stabilize()* it checks if successor's predecessor x, recently added to the network, should replace n's successor. Also, *stabilize()* updates the successor's predecessor to n, if n recently joined the network and it is the closest known predecessor of s. Periodically, in case of failure, the predecessor is set null, allowing future updating by notify method. The procedure *build_fingers()* periodically updates the routing tables.

```
// ask a node n to find k's successor
n.find_successor(k)
    if (k in (n,n.successor])
        return n.successor;
    else
        n'= closest_preceding_finger(k);
        return n'.find_successor(k);

// return closest finger preceding k
n.closest_preceding_finger(k)
    for i = m downto 1
        if(finger[i] in (n,k))
            return finger[i];
    return n;
```

Fig. 5. Look-up algorithm

A stable network is a network where $predecessor(successor(u)) = u$ is true for any node u. The pseudo-code for node joins and stabilization is presented in Fig. 4. A strong stable network is a stable network with the following property: for each node u, there is no node v on the identifier circle between u and $successor(u)$.

With minor changes in procedures presented in Figs. 4 and 5, Chord protocol is robust in case of node failures. For each node we may store a list of its first r successors. If *find_successor* fails, the lookup procedure is resumed after a timeout, passing the query to the next successor in the list. A query will not succeed only if all r successors fail. Maintaining a list of successors (at least 2) is also useful in strong-stabilizing the network. Handling node failures and strong-stabilization will be introduced in the next version of AGAPIA-Chord implementation.

Agapia Implementation of Chord. The main program *Main*, controls the node joins and failures and the communication between nodes. The functionality of a node is implemented by the module *Node*. Each node is identified by a *nodeId*. Method invocations/results are stored in a temporal array of messages containing methods arguments/results and informations about the sender and the receiver. Each method is treated in a submodule of block *Node*.

```
1.  module Main{listen nodeId, fingerSize}{read nill}
2.  {
3.      Init $ while_st(true)(
4.          ResetCounters #
5.          for_s(k=1;k< nrNodes;k++,nodeId=rNodeIds.[k])
6.              (if (randStay())
7.                      (if (rand(new())) (Node # Join);
8.                      else Node;)
9.              else Leave)
```

```
10. }
11. {speak Querys, Counters}{write nodes}
```

We use the following types:

```
1. node: (nodeId, idSuccessor, idPredecessor, fingers[]);
2. nodeIds: nodeId[]; nodes: node[];
3. qFindSuccessor: (idSnd, idRcv, Key)[];
4. rFindSuccessor: (idSnd, idRcv, Key, Result)[];
5. qGetPredecessor: (idSnd, idRcv)[];
6. rGetPredecessor: (idSnd, idRcv, idPredecessor)[];
7. qNotify: (inSnd,idRcv)[];
8. Querys: (qFindSuccessor, rFindSuccessor,
        qGetPredecessor, rGetPredecessor, qNotify);
9. Counters: (nodeId, rNodeIds, nodeIds,
        nrNodes, fingerSize);
```

The notations used to refer the components of a spatial variable X are: X.k, X.[k], X@k, X@[k] for the components of a tuple within a process, the components of an iterated tuple within a process, the k process in a tuple of processes, the k process in an iterated tuple of processes respectively. The notations are similar for temporal variables.

A spatial variable *node*, stores the attributes of an object of type node. For each lookup request, a tuple in the temporal set *qFindSuccessor* records the sender, the receiver and the searched key. The results are sent in *rFindSuccessor*. The argument of notify method always coincides with the id of the sender, hence only the id of the sender and the id of the receivers are needed.

The finger size, the number of nodes and the list of running nodes (*rNodeIds*) are stored in a temporal variable, *Counters*. The array *nodeIds* records the nodes that stay/join in the network and is used in module *ResetCounters* to update *rNodeIds*.

```
1.  module ResetCounters{listen Querys, Counters}{read nill}
2.  {
3.      Counters.nrNodes = Counters.nodeIds.length();
4.      Counters.rNodeIds = Counters.nodeIds;
5.      Counters.nodeIds = emptyset;
6.  }
7.  {speak Querys, Counters}{write nill}
```

The module *Init* creates the first node in the system, identified by *nodeId* and initialize counters and the list of messages.

```
1.  module Init{listen nodeId, fingerSize}{read nill}
2.  {
3.      node n; n.nodeId = nodeId;
```

```
4.       node.idSuccessor = nodeId;
5.       node.idPredecessor = nodeId;
6.       Querys = (emptyset,emptyset,emptyset,
7.                        emptyset,emptyset);
8.       Counters.fingerSize = fingerSize;
9.       Counters.nodeIds = {nodeId};
10.    }
11.    {speak Querys, Counters}{write node}
```

The module *Join* start a processes for a new node, acting as a constructor. Its input *jnode*, represents the id of the node that will be queried for the new node's successor. The module Leave erase the node from the nodes list.

```
1.    module Join{listen Querys, Counters}{read nill}
2.    {
3.        node n; n.nodeId = rand(fingerSize);
4.        n.idPredecessor = nill;
6.        jnode = Counters.nodeId;
7.        qFindSuccessor Union (n.nodeId, jnode, n.nodeId);
8.        nodeIds = nodeIds Union n.nodeId;
10.    {speak Querys, Counters}{write node}
11.
12.    module Leave{listen Querys, Counters}{read node}
13.    {null;}
14.    {speak Querys, Counters}{write nill}
```

All the methods executed by a node are encapsulated in module *Node*. The role of *Scatter* module is to filter the input job stream and send only the necessary arguments to each method module. The module *Gather* is used to collect the output job streams.

```
1.    module Node{listen Querys, Counters}{read node}
2.    {
3.        Scatter
4.           (BuildFingers
5.            Stabilize
6.            CheckPredecessor
7.            Notify
8.            FindSuccessor
9.            GetPredecessor
10.           GetQuerys)
11.        Gather
12.    {speak Querys, Counters}{write node}
13.
14.    module Scatter{listen  Querys, Counters}{read nill}
15.    {
16.        id = est.Counters.nodeid;
17.        qFindSuccessorN = emptyset; rFindSuccessorN = emptyset;
```

```
18.      qGetPredecessorN = emptyset;
19.      for_each((idSnd,idRcv,Key,Result) in rFindSuccessor)
20.        if (idRcv == id)
21.           rFindSuccessorN Union (idSnd, idRcv, Key, Result);
22.      for_each((idSnd,idRcv,Key) in qFindSuccessor)
23.        if (idRcv == id)
24.           qFindSuccessorN Union (idSnd, idRcv, Key);
25.      for_each((idSnd,idRcv,idPredecessor) in rGetPredecessor)
26.        if (idRcv == id)
27.           {stabNode = idPredecessor; idS = idSnd;}
28.      for_each((idSnd, idRcv) in qGetPredecessor)
29.        if (idRcv == id)
30.           {qGetPredecessorN Union (idSnd, id);}
31.      for_each((idSnd, idRcv) in qNotify)
32.        if (idRcv == id)
33.           notifyNode = idSnd;
34.      w@1 = rFindSuccessorN;
35.      w@2 = stabNode;
36.      w@3 = est.Counters.nodeIds;
37.      w@4.nodeId = notifyNode;
38.      w@5.rFindSuccessor = rFindSuccessorN;
39.      w@5.qFindSuccessor = qFindSuccessorN;
40.      w@6.qGetPredecessor = qGetPredecessorN;
41.      w@7.qFindSuccessor = qFindSuccessor Minus qFindSuccessorN;
42.      w@7.rFindSuccessor = rFindSuccessor Minus  rFindSuccessorN;
43.      w@7.qGetPredecessor = qGetPredecessor Minus qGetPredecessorN;
44.      w@7.rGetPredecessor = rGetPredecessor Minus (idS, id, stabNode);
45.      w@7.qNotify = qNotify Minus (notifyNode, id);
46.      w@7.Counters = est.Counters;
47. }
48. {speak rFindSuccessor; nodeId; nodeId[]; nodeId;
49.   (rFindSuccessor, qFindSuccessor); qGetPredecessor;
50.   (Querys, Counters)}{write nill}
51.
52. module FindSuccessor{listen rFindSuccessor, qFindSuccessor}{read  node}
53. {
54.     qFindSuccessorN = emptyset; rFindSuccessorN = emptyset;
55.     for_each (idSnd, idRcv, Key) in qFindSuccessor
56.        if(Key > nodeId  && Key <= idSuccessor){
57.           rFindSuccessorN Union (nodeId, idSnd, Key, idSuccessor);
58.        }
59.        else{
60.           cPrecNod = closest_preceding_node(Key, node.finger);
61.           qFindSuccessorN Union (nodeId, cPrecNod, Key);
62.         }
63.     for each (idSnd, idRcv, Key, Result) in rFindSuccessor
64.                 print(Result " is the successor of " + Key);
65. {speak qFindSuccessorN, rFindSuccessorN}{write node}
66.
67. module  BuildFingers{listen rFindSuccessor}{read node}
```

```
68.  {
69.      qFindSuccessorN = emptyset;
70.      for_each (idSnd, idRcv, Key, Result) in rFindSuccessor{
71.        if (Key == nodeId) idSuccessor = Result;
72.        for (i=0;i<fingers.length();i++)
73.                if (Key - nodeId == 2^i)
74.                        fingers[i] = Result;
75.      }
76.      if (randFixFingers()){
77.        for(i=0;i<fingerSize;i++)
78.                qFindSuccessorN Union (nodeId,idSuccessor, nodeId + 2^i);
79.  {speak qFindSuccessorN}{write node}
80.
81.  module Stabilize{listen stabNode: nodeId}{read node}
81.  { qGetPredecessor = emptyset; qNotifyN = emptyset;
83.    if (stabNode){
84.        if(stabNode > nodeId && stabNode < idSuccessor){
86.                idSuccessor = stabNode;
87.                qNotifyN Union (nodeId, stabNode) ;
88.        }
89.    }
90.    if (randStab())
91.        qGetPredecessorN Union (nodeId, idSuccessor);
92.  }
93.  {speak qNotifyN, qGetPredecessor}{write node}
94.
95.  module Notify{listen notifyNode: nodeId}{read node}
96.  {
97.      if (notifyNode)
98.        if(node.idPredecessor==nill ||
99.            notifyNode>node.predecessor &&  notifyNode<nodeId))
100.            node.idPredecessor = notifyNode;
101. }
102. {speak nill}{write node}
103.
104. module CheckPredecessor {listen l: nodeId[]}{read node}
105. {
106.    if (idPredecessor not in l)
107.        idPredecessor = nill;
108. }
109. {speak nill}{write node}
110.
111. module GetQuerys{listen Querys, Counters}{read node}
112. {
113.    while (Key=randKey()){
114.        qFindSuccessor Union (nodeId, nodeId, Key)
115.    }
116. }
117. {speak Querys, Counters}{write node}
118.
```

```
119. module Gather{listen qFindSuccessor; (qNotify, qGetPredecessor);
120.     nill;nill;(qFindSuccessor, rFindSuccessor); rGetPredecessor;
121.     (Querys;Counters)}{read nill}
122. {
123.     est@1 = west7.Querys Union west@1 Union west@2
124.             Union west@5 Union West@6;
125.     est@2 = west7.Counters;
126. }
127. {speak Querys, Counters}{write nill}
```

4   Conclusions and Future Work

In this paper we show an implementation of the Chord peer to peer protocol in a new programming language, named AGAPIA, introduced by Stefanescu [5–9,15,16]. The implementation aims to illustrate the expressiveness of the language and to give a better understanding of its capabilities.

There is still a lot of work to be done in this research area. A short term goal is to carry out specification and verification studies for AGAPIA programming language. Also, it would be interesting to find other possible applications for rv-systems.

Since rv-systems are constructed from finite interactive systems and the finite interactive systems accept 2-dimensional languages, of independent interest is the study of these 2-dimensional languages. There are already a few models for parallel computation based on regular expressions, for example the regular expressions extensions for Petri nets and for time automata. However, both are based on renaming and intersection, two questionable operations. Therefore, it would be extremely interesting if one could prove a Kleene theorem for regular 2-dimensional languages.

References

1. Agha, G.: Actors: A Model of Concurrent Computation in Distributed Systems. MIT Press, Cambridge (1986)
2. Arbab, F.: Reo: a channel-based coordination model for component composition. Math. Struct. Comput. Sci. **14**(3), 329–366 (2004)
3. Banu-Demergian, I.T.: The study of interaction in computing systems. Ph.D. thesis, University of Bucharest (2014)
4. Broy, M., Olderog, E.R.: Trace-oriented models of concurrency. In: Bergstra, J.A., et al. (eds.) Handbook of Process Algebra, pp. 101–196. North-Holland, Amsterdam (2001)
5. Dragoi, C., Stefanescu, G.: Structured programming for interactive rv-systems. IMAR Preprint 9/2006, Bucharest (2006)
6. Dragoi, C., Stefanescu, G.: Implementation and verification of ring termination detection protocols using structured rv-programs. Ann. Univ. Bucharest Math. Inform. Ser. **55**, 129–138 (2006)

7. Dragoi, C., Stefanescu, G.: AGAPIA v0.1: a programming language for interactive systems and its typing system. In: Proceedings of the FINCO 2007, ETAPS Workshop on the Foundations of Interactive Computation, Braga, Portugal. ENTCS Volume, pp. 61–76 (2007, in press)

8. Dragoi, C., Stefanescu, G.: AGAPIA v0.1: a programming language for interactive systems and its typing systems. In: Proceedings of the FINCO/ETAPS 2007 (2007). ENTCS Vol. **203**(3), 69–94 (2008)

9. Dragoi, C., Stefanescu, G.: On spatio-temporal logics for the verification of structured interactive programs with registers and voice. In: WADT 2008, 19th International Workshop on Algebraic Development Techniques, Pisa, Italy, 13–16 June (2008)

10. Gadducci, F., Montanari, U.: The tile model. In: Proof, Language, and Interaction: Essays in Honor of Robin Milner, pp. 133–168. MIT Press (1999)

11. Goldin, D., Smolka, S., Wegner, P. (eds.): Interactive Computation: The New Paradigm. Springer, Heidelberg (2006)

12. Kavalionak, H., Montresor, A.: P2P and cloud: a marriage of convenience for replica management. In: Kuipers, F.A., Heegaard, P.E. (eds.) IWSOS 2012. LNCS, vol. 7166, pp. 60–71. Springer, Heidelberg (2012)

13. Milner, R.: Communicating and Mobile Systems: The Pi Calculus. Cambridge University Press, Cambridge (1999)

14. Misra, J., Cook, W.: Computation Orchestration. Softw. Syst. Model. **6**(1), 83–110 (2007)

15. Popa, A., Sofronia, A., Stefanescu, G.: High-level structured interactive programs with registers and voices. J. Univ. Comput. Sci. **13**(11), 1722–1754 (2007)

16. Popa, A., Sofronia, A., Stefanescu, G.: Undecidability results for finite interactive systems. In: Proceedings of the SYNASC 2008, pp. 366–369 (2008)

17. Stefanescu, G.: Interactive systems with registers and voices. Fundamenta Informaticae **73**, 285–306 (2006)

18. Stoica, I., et al.: Chord: a scalable peer-to-peer lookup protocol for internet applications. IEEE/ACM Trans. Netw. **11**(1), 17–32 (2003)

19. Jensen, O.H., Milner, R.: Bigraphs and transitions. In: Proceedings of the POPL 2003, pp. 38–49 (2003)

20. Wadge, W., Ashcroft, E.A.: Lucid, the Dataflow Programming Language. Academic Press, New York (1985)

21. Wegner, P.: Interactive foundations of computing. Theor. Comput. Sci. **192**, 315–351 (1998)

Multiscale Blood Vessel Segmentation in Retinal Fundus Images Algorithm Implementation and Analysis

Aigerim Sarbasova and Md. Mahmud Hasan[✉]

Department of IT & MM, International IT University,
34A Manas 8A Dzhandossova Street, Almaty 050040, Kazakhstan
m.hasam@iitu.kz

Abstract. Image segmentation helps to analyze images by simplifying the representation of image. It is clear that there is no universal algorithm for image segmentation methods; different methods should be used depending on the application. In this paper multiscale blood vessel segmentation in retinal fundus images algorithm [1] was implemented and its parts were analyzed. In order to reduce noise, OpenCV blurring functions were used. Moreover, the problem of segmentation was described. It was observed that the blood vessel can be identified using the multiscale blood vessel segmentation in retinal fundus images algorithm. It also found that the preprocessing of the captured fundus images is very essential. Thus the results can be further enhanced by using selective and regional image smoothing functions according to the fundus images characteristics before applying the multiscale blood vessel segmentation in retinal fundus images algorithm.

Keywords: Image segmentation · Medical image analysis · Blood vessel segmentation

1 Introduction

Image analysis has been playing an important role in the computer aided identification of ophthalmologic disorders. Various types of ophthalmologic disorders are related with retinal vasculatures. Retinal fundus blood vessels exploration helps to find out eye diseases, like glaucoma and diabetic retinopathy. The fundus is the only part of the human body where both the circulation and the nerve tissue can be inspected non-invasively. A fundus photograph is an image of the fundus taken by an ophthalmoscope, or a fundus camera.

Fundus photography is still the most cost-effective image modality clinically. It is also commonly used in screening programs, where the photos can be analyzed later for diagnosis and be used to monitor the progress in many diseases. In a screening program, where thousands of fundus photographs are taken, it is impossible for the ophthalmologists to personally exam every photo, especially in the extremely laborious work such as measuring vessel width for every vessel segment.

Nowadays doctors can diagnose diseases by retina observation. For example, researchers in UK created the Portable Eye Examination Kit, which makes photos of

© Springer International Publishing Switzerland 2015
R. Horne (Ed.): EGC 2015, CCIS 514, pp. 113–121, 2015.
DOI: 10.1007/978-3-319-25043-4_11

the back of retina. This photo is sent to doctor for check [3]. As it is time consuming and inefficient operation to process images manually, there is a strong need in automatic segmentation methods. One of the difficult problems in image processing is image segmentation. Segmentation is the process of dividing an image into regions with similar properties such as gray level, color, texture, brightness, and contrast [2]. Presence of stochastic processes, such as texture, texton, stochastic point, line, curve, graph, regions makes the task of segmentation more complex. For many applications, segmentation reduces to finding an object in an image. This involves partitioning the image into two class of regions - either object or background. There are numerous ways to model a blood vessel, but we have chosen to think of a vessel as a collection of lines and edges [8]. Methods to detect lines, edges, structures in images are:

- Masking/filtering
- Gradient operators
- Laplacian operators
- Hessian operators.

Segmentation is taking place naturally in the human visual system. We are experts on detecting patterns, lines, edges and shapes, and making decisions based upon the visual information. At the same time, we are overwhelmed by the amount of image information that can be captured by today's technology [8].

There are a lot of methods for image segmentation of retinal fundus images using different techniques and algorithms, like histogram equalization and automatic threshold selection [10], fully-connected CRFs training [11], tight frames [12], Star Networked Pixel Tracking [13].

This research considers presenting clear, fast and accurate multiscale vessel segmentation algorithm that can segment the vessels for visual analysis, suggested in [1]. This algorithm has the capability to detect the vessels faster with high accuracy. Furthermore, step by step application of image processing techniques resulting the vessel enhancement, which is the key to the retinal fundus analysis. In this paper the algorithm of blood vessel segmentation in retinal fundus images is implemented and analyzed by the OpenCV library.

2 Multiscale Blood Vessel Segmentation in Retinal Fundus Images Algorithm

There are two main techniques, which are used for segmentation images of retinas into portions that are blood vessels and not blood vessels. One technique is a window based method. This involves looking at a small region of the image and extracting possible blood vessel pixels based on local image characteristics. Another methodology involves exploiting the known structure of veins and arteries to evaluate potential vessels [9].

The characteristic of retinal image is a vessel tree with optic nerve creating a binary map. In general the retinal fundus images are telecentric and this allows the lens to be focused to different distances without changing the size of the high resolution retinal fundus images. (1) The preprocessing step the acceptable contrast between the vessels and the background should be established. From the RGB image, it is essetial to extract the green channel, because Green channel has high intensity as compared to Red and Blue. Here for this algorithm, a 3 level of Gaussian pyramid has been applied to the image. The resulting image is a low pass filtered version of the original image. (2) To identify the curvature of the image from the neighborhood analysis a second-order partial derivatives of a function (Hessian matrix) need to be executed. (3) Final it is essential to threshold the image for the vessel tracking. In this stage it is also possible to enhance the image for several purposes, like visual inspection, computerized vessel counting and identification.

Thus the final algorithm is in 3 stages:

1. Green channel is extracted and 3 level of Gaussian pyramid are generated
2. Neighborhood analysis is made on each level with Hessian matrix
3. The threshold is applied and results are merged with bitwise or operator.

3 Algorithm Implementation

3.1 Green Channel is Extracted and 3 Level of Gaussian Pyramid are Generated

To get only green channel from the image, image is split to 3 constituent channels. Then to red and blue parts of image are assigned to zero matrixes. After that, the image again merged.

$$g = G/(R + G + B) \tag{1}$$

In this equation g is a Green channel and R, G and B are Red, Green and Blue channels respectively.

split(src1, channel);

```
Mat pyrs0, pyrs1, pyrs2;
Channel [0] = Mat::zeros (src1.rows, src1.cols,
CV_8UC1);
Channel [2] = Mat::zeros (src1.rows, src1.cols, CV_8UC1);
merge(channel, 3, pyrs0);
```

In other channel pictures the vessels are not noticeable as in green channel image. So, it can be said, that by eliminating other channels, except green; some part of noise is removed. After taking out only green channel, standard OpenCV's pyrDown operation is made (Fig. 1).

```
pyrDown (pyrs0, pyrs1, Size (pyrs0.cols/2, pyrs0.rows/2));
pyrDown (pyrs1, pyrs2, Size (pyrs1.cols/2, pyrs1.rows/2));
```

Now there are 3 levels of pyramids. They look similar but their sizes differ twice from each other.

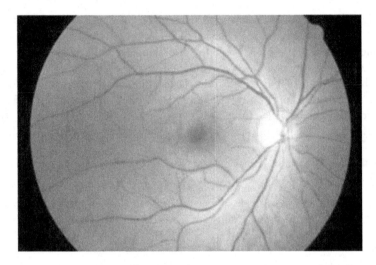

Fig. 1. Original image of retinal fundus [4] (Color figure online)

3.2 Neighborhood Analysis is Made on Each Level with Hessian Matrix

An image may be defined as two dimensional light intensity function f(x, y) where x and y denote spatial co-ordinate and the amplitude or value of f at any point (x, y) is called intensity or grayscale or brightness of the image at that point.

It is essential to identify the curvature of the image. That has been done by the Hessian matrix operation that performed the neighborhood analysis using the second order partial derivatives of a function. The Hessian matrix of second derivatives is calculated for all 3 levels of pyramid (Fig. 2).

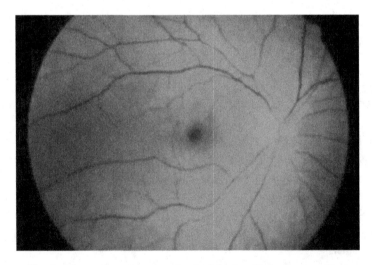

Fig. 2. Green channel image of retinal fundus (Color figure online)

$$H(\mathrm{f}) = \begin{pmatrix} \frac{\partial^2 f}{\partial^2 x} & \frac{\partial^2 f}{\partial x \partial y} \\ \frac{\partial^2 f}{\partial x \partial y} & \frac{\partial^2 f}{\partial^2 y} \end{pmatrix} \qquad (2)$$

```
res0 = hesManipulation (pyrs0);
res1 = hesManipulation (pyrs1);
res2 = hesManipulation (pyrs2);
```

In order to find out second order diffential the formula for high order differentiation is used:

$$f''(x) = y_i'' \approx \frac{y_{i+1} - 2y_{i+y_{i-1}}}{h^2} \qquad (3)$$

Where, h is increment in x direction in evenly spaced grid of points. Here it is value will be equal to 1. y_i - value of function in definite point, y_{i+1} and y_{i-1}- values of function in neighboring positions.

```
double dxx = pyr.at <Vec3b> (Point(i + 1, j)).val[1] - 2 *
pyr.at < Vec3b > (Point(i, j)).val[1] + pyr.at <Vec3b> (Point
(i - 1, j)).val[1];
double dyy = pyr.at <Vec3b> (Point(i, j + 1)).val[1] - 2 *
pyr.at <Vec3b> (Point(i, j)).val[1] +
pyr.at <Vec3b> (Point(i, j - 1)).val[1];
double dxy = 1/4 * (pyr.at <Vec3b> (Point(i + 1, j +
1)).val[1] - pyr.at <Vec3b> (Point(i + 1, j 1)).val[1] -
pyr.at <Vec3b> (Point(i - 1, j + 1)).val[1] +
pyr.at <Vec3b> (Point(i - 1, j - 1)).val[1]);
```

Eigenvalue of found Hessian matrix is found by using formula:

$$A - \lambda I = 0 \qquad (4)$$

In this formula A – calculated Hessian matrix, λ - eigenvalue (characteristic vector), I – identity matrix. In order to find eigenvalue of hessian matrix at each point, quadratic equation is solved. The resulted pixel in given position is calculated with formula.

$$P_{vessel} = 1 - \frac{a_l}{a_h} \qquad (5)$$

Where,
a_l – lower eigenvalue
a_h – higher eigenvalue

The result is assigned to green channel of the image, values for other channel are 0. After applying hessian matrix, downscaled images are returned to previous size.

```
pyrUp (res1, res1, Size(src.cols, src.rows));
pyrUp (res2, res2, Size(src.cols/2, src.rows/2));
pyrUp (res2, res2, Size(src.cols, src.rows));
```

3.3 The Threshold is Applied and Results are Merged with Bitwise or Operator

All images are binarized applying a hysteresis threshold, where the two thresholds are set to 85 % and 93 % (Fig. 3).

```
res0 = applyThreshold(res0);
res1 = applyThreshold(res1);
res2 = applyThreshold(res2);
```

Hysteresis threshold algorithm is applied. The algorithm uses 2 thresholds, Thigh and Tlow (Fig. 4).

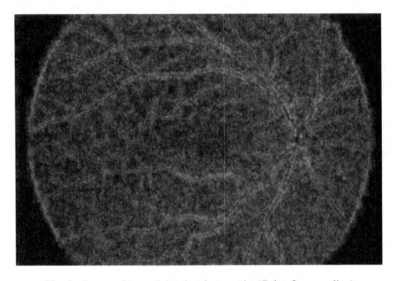

Fig. 3. Image after applying hessian matrix (Color figure online)

```
A pixel (x; y) is called strong if f(x; y) > Thigh.
A pixel (x; y) is called weak if f(x; y) < Tlow.
All other pixels are called candidate pixels.
```

1. In each position of (x; y), discard the pixel (x; y) if it is weak; output the pixel if it is strong.
2. If the pixel is a candidate, follow the chain of connected local maxima in both directions along the edge, as long as f(x,y) > Tlow.
3. If the starting candidate pixel (x; y) is connected to a strong pixel, output this candidate pixel; otherwise, do not output the candidate pixel [5].

Hysteresis threshold removed some noise, as it can be seen from picture. All pictures were merged with bitwise or operator. For more comfort picture was converted to grayscale [6, 7].

Fig. 4. Image after applying hysteresis Threshold (Color figure online)

```
bitwise_or(res0, res1, dst);
bitwise_or(dst, res2, dst1);
dst1 = dst;
cvtColor(dst1, dst1, CV_RGB2GRAY);
```

In order to reduce noise in more extent, it was decided to use smoothing operations. Applying smoothing operations at the end of the algorithm worsened result. Applying standard OpenCV blur and GaussianBlur functions before the algorithm improved

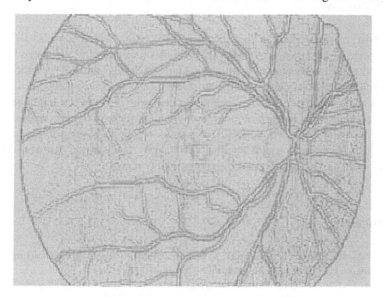

Fig. 5. Image after merging and gray scaling

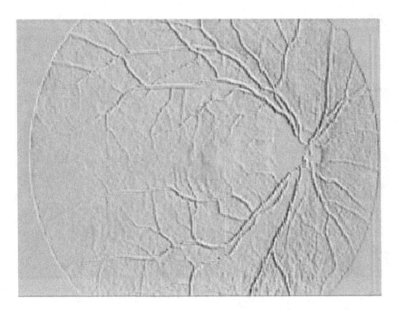

Fig. 6. 3D perspective image enhancement (Color figure online).

result similarly, while using of medianBlur and bilateralFilter didn't change anything (Fig. 5).

After some visual enhancement the image can be look like the Fig. 6, in 3d perspective.

4   Conclusion

The purpose of this algorithm to enhancement of retinal blood vessels. To do that image processing techniques has been used. In this paper method presented is multi-scale blood vessel segmentation in retinal fundus images algorithm. The algorithm has been developed and implemented by the OpenCV. The main achievement of this method is it's less computational processing vs competitively accurate compared to the other segmentation techniques. It was found out that the obtained results can be improved by using selective smoothing functions before algorithm. It was observed that, we can have some useful results, if we apply this simple, fast and accurate algorithm over the infected area of the retinal blood vessels.

References

1. Budai, A., Michelson, G., Hornegger, J.: Multiscale Blood Vessel. http://www5.informatik. unierlangen.de/Forschung/Publikationen/2010/Budai10-MBV.pdf
2. Ivanov, I.: CV in Medical Imaging (2013). http://webee.technion.ac.il/~lihi/Teaching/ 2012_winter_048921/PPT/Igor.pdf

3. Macdonald, F.: This device turns your phone into an eye exam machine. http://www. sciencealert.com/watch-this-device-turns-your-phone-into-an-eyeexam-machine
4. High-Resolution Fundus (HRF) Image Database. https://www5.cs.fau.de/research/data/ fundus-images/
5. Cserverikov, D.: Basic Algorithms for Digital Image Analysis. http://progmat.uw.hu/oktseg/ kepelemzes/lec06_edge_4.pdf
6. Yound, T., Mohlenkamp, M.J.: Introduction to Numerical Methods and Matlab Programming for Engineers, Chapter 7
7. OpenCV documentation. http://docs.opencv.org/
8. Läthén, G.: Segmentation Methods for Medical Image Analysis (2010). http://liu.diva-portal. org/smash/get/diva2:310036/FULLTEXT02.pdf
9. Echevarria, P., Miller, T., O'Meara, J.: Blood Vessel Segmentation in Retinal Images (2004). http://robots.stanford.edu/cs223b04/inter2/P14.pdf
10. Saleh, M.D., Eswaran, C., Mueen, A.: An automated blood vessel segmentation algorithm using histogram equalization and automatic threshold selection. J. Digit. Imaging **24**(4), 564–572 (2011). http://www.ncbi.nlm.nih.gov/pubmed/20524139
11. Orlando, J.I., Blaschko, M.: Learning fully-connected CRFs for blood vessel segmentation in retinal images. In: Golland, P., Hata, N., Barillot, C., Hornegger, J., Howe, R. (eds.) MICCAI 2014, Part I. LNCS, vol. 8673, pp. 634–641. Springer, Heidelberg (2014). https:// hal.inria.fr/hal-01024226/document
12. Cai, X., Chan, R., Morigi, S., Sgallari, F.: Vessel segmentation in medical imaging using a tight-frame-based algorithm. SIAM J. Imaging Sci. **6**(1), 464–486 (2013). http://epubs.siam. org/doi/abs/10.1137/110843472
13. Ocbagabir, H., Hameed, I., Abdulmalik, S., Buket, D.B.: A novel vessel segmentation algorithm in color images of the retina (2013). http://ieeexplore.ieee.org/xpl/login.jsp?tp= &arnumber=6578224&url=http%3A%2F%2Fieeexplore.ieee.org%2Fxpls%2Fabs_all.jsp% 3Farnumber%3D6578224

Generating Mediators for Dynamic Interoperability Across Cloud Providers

Oleg Trubitsin[✉]

Faculty of Information Technology, Kazakh-British Technical University,
Almaty, Kazakhstan
olegtrubitsin@gmail.com

Abstract. With the growing popularity of cloud computing and large number of providers, it is necessary to select the most appropriate service. To select a suitable provider the user needs to browse a huge list of providers. To solve this problem, the customer can use a third-party service called a cloud broker. One of the problem we faced during the developing cloud broker framework is a lack of API standards. Every provider has its own protocol for deploying services. This paper describes a new approach to construct a protocol for communication between the client and the provider. It is based on the use of mediators, which, depending on the selected service capable to convert messages from a format of one particular provider to a format of another provider. All the processes described in a specific example of Google Compute Engine client and Digital Ocean server interactions for deploying the service. In addition, during the development of mediators was introduced a new operator "sync" to synchronize the set of answers to one.

Keywords: Cloud broker · Cloud computing · Apache Jclouds · Starlink · Mediator · Cloud provider

1 Introduction

Due to the fast-emerging cloud computing market the number of cloud providers have significantly increased. The customer is faced with the problem of choosing a suitable service. First of all, the user is looking for a provider that would satisfy his requirements including cost and reliability. Thus, the customers have to decide about cloud to choose in order to meet their functional and non-functional service requirements.

L. Frank Kenney "The future of cloud computing will be permeated with the notion of brokers negotiating relationships between providers of cloud services and the service customers. In this context, a broker might be software, appliances, platforms or suites of technologies that enhance the base services available through the cloud. Enhancement will include managing access to these services, providing greater security or even creating completely new services" [1].

© Springer International Publishing Switzerland 2015
R. Horne (Ed.): EGC 2015, CCIS 514, pp. 122–133, 2015.
DOI: 10.1007/978-3-319-25043-4_12

A precise description is given in publication of National Institute of Standards and Technology (NIST) [2]: "A cloud broker is an entity that manages the use, performance and delivery of cloud services and negotiates relationships between cloud providers and cloud consumers".

In this paper, we present a new approach for enabling dynamic interoperability between of cloud providers. The main idea lies in using mediators as a middleware between the customer and provider of services. The protocol for mediator was developed using an extension of the Scribble language [3]. The extension is a synchronization operator, which depending on received messages gives an opportunity to merge answers from the server into one common response.

The paper is organized as follows: Sect. 2 briefly explains the main differences between two cloud providers and the idea of using mediators based on Apache Jclouds [4] and Starlink [5]. Section 3 presents a process of developing a protocol for mediators using Scribble. Finally, Sect. 4 concludes the paper and briefly discusses related work.

2   Comparison of Digital Ocean and Google Compute Engine APIs

In the following, lack of API's standards for cloud providers is the major problem for cloud customers. As different providers offer different APIs it is very hard to develop an application which will be suitable for all of them. Each cloud provider has its own API, each of which provides different services.

For example, APIs of Digital Ocean and Google Compute Engine[1] shows difference in provided services. For such existing operations cloud broker needs a mediator as middleware between clients and cloud providers.

DigitalOcean provides 10 predefined plans. The only choice which a customer can choose is the region of location of the cloud, OS and opportunity of enabling the backup service. The Google Compute Engine provides much more operations such as standard VM deployment, load balancing, creating the buckets, software installation, location and etc.

2.1   Apache Jclouds as a Mediator

One of the solutions is to use Apache Jclouds[2] as a mediator between cloud broker and cloud provider [6]. Jclouds is a multi-cloud toolkit for the Java platform. The API gives an opportunity to use portable abstractions or cloud-specific features. It supports more than 30 cloud providers such as Amazon WebServices, Google Compute Engine, Rackspace, Amazon S3 and Microsoft Azure[3].

Jclouds allows to write code that will be applicable to all providers. And depending on the arguments passed, will deploy a service that the customer

---

[1] DigitalOcean API, https://developers.digitalocean.com/v1/ and Google Compute Engine, https://cloud.google.com/compute/.

[2] Apache Jclouds official page, http://jclouds.apache.org/.

[3] Apache Jclouds providers, http://jclouds.apache.org/reference/providers/.

```
"status":  "OK",
"droplets":  [
   {
      "id":  100823,
      "name":  "test222",
      "image_id":  420,
      "size_id":33,
      "region_id":  1,
      "backups_active":  false,
      "ip_address":  "127.0.0.1",
      "private_ip_address":  null,
      "locked":  false,
      "status":  "active",
      "created_at":  "2015−02−11T09:30:00Z"
   }
]
}
```

Fig. 1. Example of DigitalOcean JSON message

requires. Writing code for each provider separately is expensive, exhaustive and error-prone process. As mentioned above, there is no single standard API for providers. Each has its own set of specifications that are available to the user. All of the available libraries for cloud providers were developed jointly with the providers [6].

Browsing of services to find any that meets user's requirements includes the following steps. Firstly, the customer sends technical details of the cloud which he wants to get. Technical details includes such information as operating system, size of RAM, disk space (as another scenario, the customer wants to connect his VM with another data storage, for example with Amazon S3), location and availability of load balancing. The cloud broker searches for suitable providers and when the providers found the service sends information to the customer. If the user accepts the results, the broker starts to deploy the service. In our case the service fill in the arguments with parameters (provider, OS, cloud plans, additional services). Next steps include extracting of the code by mediator. All of these steps are shown in sequence diagram Fig. 2. If the termination completes successfully, all the information will be send to the cloud broker and by this time will be available in the web-interface of the cloud broker service. Anytime the customer can add or delete services. The process of adding or deleting again sends to the mediator.

2.2 Starlink for Composing Protocols

According to the above one may assume that Jclouds solves the problem with a heterogeneity of API of cloud providers. But Jclouds does not solve the dynamic interoperability of these protocols. And as said above, Jclouds supports a few

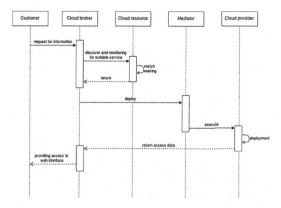

Fig. 2. Sequence diagram for Cloud broker

amount of providers. But what if a customer chooses a service not presented in API of Apache Jclouds? In this case he will loose opportunity to get this service.

As mentioned earlier, Intercloud [7,8] is a "globally interconnected Clouds" [9]. This means that customer could choose different providers which have different APIs. It would be very complex to create an application which will be suitable for the most requirements. Suppose a customer wants to combine DigitalOcean services with services offered by Google Compute Engine. The client may try to deploy services by sending requests, which are incompatible on other provider. In this case, the client will have to rewrite the application.

Starlink [10] framework allows an interoperability solution to be specified using domain specific languages that are then used to generate the necessary executable software to enable runtime interoperability.

In [11], Bromberg et al. show on example of Picasa and Flickr APIs how using the Starlink framework we can solve the problem of interoperability of protocols. The solution lays on creating mediators to provide dynamic composition of existing systems. According to [11] to overcome the combined application and middleware heterogeneity, propose two key requirements. First, mediators that act as interoperability enablers must be automatically generated and dynamically deployed. Second, middleware protocol migration and API evolutions must be handled with minimal development effort. This is achieved not by developing an application but by creating a model how this services should operate. Depending on the request the suitable middleware protocol will be generated [10].

3   Scribble for Defining Cloud Broker Protocol

This section describes the process of creating mediators, based on the basic idea of Starlink [5]. The main task of the mediators in the deployment of resources is their compatibility with all providers. That is, regardless of where we want to receive the service, we do not need to rewrite the application, since mediators will be automatically generated and adjust requests for the necessary API requirements. For this purpose we leverage the protocol modeling capability of the Scribble framework.

Scribble is a language to describe interactions between multiple parties in the form of protocol. A protocol is a notion which provides an abstract description of the communication patterns and the types of messages exchanged [12].

Scribble is used for precisely describing the global behavior of a system. This is accomplished by representing the rules that indicate a certain order of actions depending on the situation.

As were described in Sect. 2, Google Compute Engine and Digital Ocean API's have significant differences and one request cannot be applied to deploying services on another cloud provider. The protocol for deploying droplets on Digital Ocean in terms of Scribble is presented below.

```
global protocol DigitalOcean (role Client,
role DigitalOcean){
        POST(token) from Client to DigitalOcean;
        GET(token) from DigitalOcean to Client;
        POST(JSON) from Client to DigitalOcean;
        choice at DigitalOcean {
          return(response) from DigitalOcean to Client;
          } or {
        alert(error) from DigitalOcean to Client;
          }
}
```

Fig. 3. Global protocol of Digital Ocean API

A global protocol in Fig. 3 represents the sequence of steps for deploying services. This helps to understand the interaction between parties: Client and Digital Ocean cloud-provider. The protocol starts with a POST(token) request from a client to server. The server responds by GET(token) message. POST(token) and GET(token) are operations which used for receiving of an authentication token. A value in parentheses represents a type of messages. These types of messages can be defined in a preamble. POST(JSON) is an operation for sending a required parameters in JSON format to the provider's URI. An example of JSON message presented in Sect. 2 in Fig. 1. The operator *choice* gives an opportunity to cloud broker to choose which operation in choice block can be perform during the request. In case of the global protocol for Digital Ocean provider it could return the response of successful deployment or return error message with the error code.

In Fig. 4, we project an example of a local protocol automatically generated from a global protocol for the Google Compute Engine. The local protocol used for describing interactions for a specific role, when the global protocol represents interactions between multiple parties. In addition, it can be used for specifying monitors, which in turn are used for dynamic validation of types and to verify

```
local  protocol  GoogleComputeEngine  at  Client(role  Client ,
role  GoogleComputeEngine ) {
        POST(token)  to  GoogleComputeEngine ;
        GET(token)  from  GoogleComputeEngine ;
        par {
                POST1(JSON)  to  GoogleComputeEngine ;
                choice  at  GoogleComputeEngine {
                        return(response)  from  GoogleComputeEngine ;
                        choice  at  Client {
                          request(abort)  to  GoogleComputeEngine
                        } or {}
                } or {
                        alert(error)  from  GoogleComputeEngine ;
                        choice  at  Client {
                          request(abort)  to  GoogleComputeEngine
                        } or {}
                }
        } and {
                POST2(JSON)  to  GoogleComputeEngine ;
                choice  at  GoogleComputeEngine {
                        return(response)  from  GoogleComputeEngine ;
                        choice  at  Client {
                          request(abort)  to  GoogleComputeEngine
                        } or {}
                } or {
                        alert(error)  from  GoogleComputeEngine ;
                        choice  at  Client {
                          request(abort)  to  GoogleComputeEngine
                        } or {}
                }
        }
}
```

Fig. 4. Local protocol of Google Compute engine client

that the message will be delivered to the destination, according to the protocol description. There is differences in contrast of Digital Ocean protocol with Google Compute Engine. For deploying two instances in Google Cloud Engine, we need to send two messages, unlike Digital Ocean where we send one message, that consist of a JSON message with required parameters for two droplets. The operator *Par* means that we start two protocols in parallel. As an extension for Scribble we add an empty choice. On example of local protocol for the Google Compute Engine client, the empty choice means that in case of error message the client could choose the abort request to the server and the operation would be aborted or choose nothing and there would be no further operations by the client. Assume the situation when one POST(JSON) operation successfully ended, but the second POST(JSON) operation ended with a problem. The client could choose request(abort) and interrupt the deployment, because of he expects two positive answers. In case of successful POST(JSON) operation the server just response by return(response) message, which means that deploy operation has been done correctly.

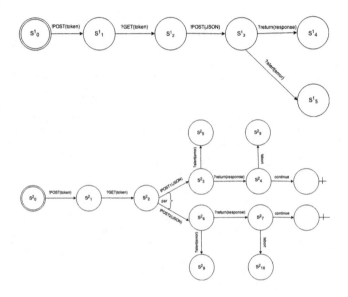

Fig. 5. Automata for Digital Ocean server and Google Compute Engine client

Automata for server and client helps clearly understand the sequence of steps for deploying the droplets. An aim of this project was to find an opportunity to deploy services, using client requests of one cloud provider, on the side of another. The automata in Fig. 5 provides a graphical view of the local protocols that must be integrate by the mediator. These automata were used to generate the automata for the mediator in Fig. 6. The client of Google Compute Engine performed the process of deploying the service on Digital Ocean server. In general, as we can see, the sequence of steps is identical in both cases, but as requests will be incomprehensible to others, we should have a link, which will transform one-request types to another. Operation of deploying droplets on Digital Ocean starts with the Google Compute Engine client's request for getting an authentication token. Using mediator we dynamically transform the client's request into server's type. Upon receiving a request from a client, the mediator transforms and transmits to the server side. The answer must also be converted into a client-friendly type. Once the token is received, we will proceed to request the deployment of services. Sent POST request containing a JSON is transformed again on the side of the mediator, and because the client does not support Google's two related JSON we parallelize this operation to several requests. As noted previously, the server decides, depending on the success of the operation to return a successful response, or to inform the client of the error. Two POST request eventually have eight of various outcomes (success-error,

error-error, expected success results and etc.). In such cases, there is a need to synchronize the responses by sync operator "S" and provides to the client only one result.

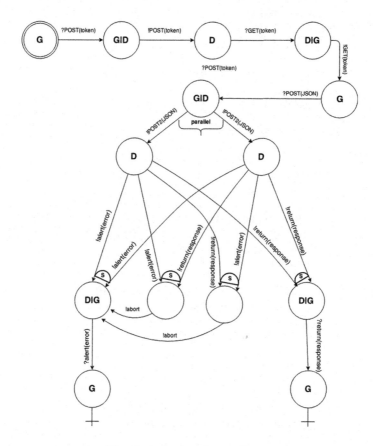

Fig. 6. Automata for mediator

Since the Scribble does not support the synchronization operation, we introduced an additional operator sync, which depending on received set of messages from the server, will synchronize them and provide to the client only one result. This operator could be described in an algebraic style using the symbol ⊗. The symbol ⊗ in our sync operation means that the two synchronised branches of the protocol are perform if and only if both are completely performed in parallel. For example, if each branch of sync is a receive message operation, then both messages must be received before the protocol can continue. We also use the symbol ⊕ as an external choice [13] that is made in reaction to two possible scenarios.

Now consider the following example expressed in an algebraic style.

$$((OK \otimes OK) \,;\, succ) \oplus (((ER \otimes ER) \oplus ((ER \otimes OK) \,;\, abort)) \,;\, fail)$$

```
local protocol mediator (role Client, role Server,
role Mediator) {
  POST(token) from Client;
  POST(token) to Server;
  GET(token) from Client;
  GET(token) to Server;
  POST(JSON) from Client;
  par {
    POST1(JSON) to Server;
    } and {
    POST2(JSON) to Server;
    }
  choice at Server{
      sync {
        alert(error) from Server;
      } and {
        alert(error) from Server;
      }
      alert(error) to Client;
  } or {
      sync {
        alert(error) from Server;
      }and{
        return(response) from Server;
        return(abort) to Server;
      }
      alert(error) to Client;
  } or {
      sync {
        return(response) from Server;
      }and{
        return(response) from Server;}
      return(response) to Client;
  }
}
```

Fig. 7. Local protocol of mediator

We can read this as: "if we receive messages OK and OK we will get a successful response. Or if there will be ER and ER or ER and OK messages we must abort operation and send fail message".

According to the algebraic style of "sync", the OK message is a return(response) and ER is a alert(error). In the protocol in Fig. 7 if the server sends two positive messages OK from two parallel operations for deploying instances, we should synchronize them into one and send success message to the client. However there are two other variants of combination of received messages, since the server has two choices of response. He can return error message ER with combination of success message OK or two error messages ER and ER. For both of these possibilities, we should also synchronize two messages and return only one fail message. In the basis of the automata in Fig. 6 was written the global protocol for mediator in terms of Scribble.

The resulting protocol in Fig. 7 repeats the sequence of steps of automata for mediator, which were described above. We send POST(token) message to the mediator which in turn transforms it to the type of server. After it he sends the request to the Digital Ocean and after receiving it, the server responds by GET(token) message. The mediator again transforms it to the client-friendly type and sends to the client. Next message POST(JSON) comes from the customer. As said above, this message consist of JSON with a set of required parameters. At this stage, there is a parallelization of operations. The mediator forwards to the server two POST1(JSON) and POST2(JSON) messages in parallel. Further, a provider has a choice. The choice consists of synchronized by sync operator messages. In case of two alert(error) messages we synchronize them and send to the client response with an error. Only in case of combination of positive and negative responses from the server the client sends an abort message and interrupt the deployment. If the server responded by two successful return(response) messages we just answer to the client by return(response). After the results are synchronized, the data are forwarded to mediator to transform the server's type of message to the Google client's type.

The main advantage of this approach, as mentioned earlier, is that we will not rewrite the entire application, but only changing patterns of interaction. In our case, we substitute the needed types of messages, related to a particular provider.

4 Conclusion and Related Work

In this paper, we proposed an approach to addressing the heterogeneity of protocols among cloud providers, inspired by Starlink [5]. The basic idea is to provide a methodology that assists in the generation of mediators that enable dynamic interoperability of protocols between the customer and multiple cloud providers. Such mediators eliminate the need to rewrite applications written for one cloud provider that must interact with other Cloud providers.

In this methodology, we generate mediators according to a specification for the APIs to be integrated. According to the specification, the mediator is designed such that it transforms the message types used for a single service provider, into types of messages of another. The result is a specification for the protocol for a mediator in the specification Scribble language. We provide an example of applying this methodology for a client migrating from DigitalOcean to the Google Compute Engine.

Due the requirements of the protocols investigated, we introduced new operators, which are not present in current implementation of Scribble [12]. For synchronization of messages, we introduce a "sync" operator indicating that the synchronised parts of the protocol is performed correctly if and only if both parts execute completely. The effect is that the synchronised parts of the protocol can be treated as a single atomic message. In addition, we add an empty response from the client in the choice operation. It is related to the fact that if there are errors, the client has a choice between interrupting the operation of service deployment and silently terminating successfully, in case of selection of empty branch of a choice.

Local protocols for mediators may be used as a specification for the construction of mediators that integrate clients with Cloud providers, thereby providing a methodology to solve the problem of the dynamic interoperability of protocols. Future work will also include a description of the formal semantics for the protocol of mediators. Based on a formal semantics, tools can be developed that will further automate the process of the generation and verification of mediators for the dynamic interoperability of heterogeneous Cloud providers.

References

1. Smith, D., Plummer, D., Cearley, D.: The what, why, and when of cloud computing. Special report. Gartner (2009)
2. Liu, F., Tong, J., Mao, J., Bohn, R., Messina, J., Badger, L., Leaf, D.: Nist cloud computing reference architecture. NIST special publication 500-292 (2011)
3. Honda, K., Mukhamedov, A., Brown, G., Chen, T.-C., Yoshida, N.: Scribbling interactions with a formal foundation. In: Natarajan, R., Ojo, A. (eds.) ICDCIT 2011. LNCS, vol. 6536, pp. 55–75. Springer, Heidelberg (2011)
4. Di Martino, B., Cretella, G., Esposito, A.: Cross-platform cloud APIs. In: Di Martino, B., et al. (eds.) Cloud Portability and Interoperability, pp. 45–57. Springer, Heidelberg (2015)
5. Bromberg, Y.D., Grace, P., Reveillere, L.: Starlink: runtime interoperability between heterogeneous middleware protocols. In: IEEE Trans 31st International Conference on Distributed Computing System, pp. 446–455 (2010)
6. Graham, S.T., Liu, X.: Critical evaluation on jclouds and cloudify abstract APIs against EC2, azure and HP-cloud. In: 2014 IEEE 38th International Computer Software and Applications Conference Workshops (COMPSACW), pp. 510–515. IEEE (2014)
7. Buyya, R., Ranjan, R., Calheiros, R.N.: Intercloud: utility-oriented federation of cloud computing environments for scaling of application services. In: Hsu, C.-H., Yang, L.T., Park, J.H., Yeo, S.-S. (eds.) ICA3PP 2010, Part I. LNCS, vol. 6081, pp. 13–31. Springer, Heidelberg (2010)
8. Grozev, N., Buyya, R.: Inter-cloud architectures and application brokering: taxonomy and survey. Softw. Pract. Experience 44(3), 369–390 (2014)
9. Bernstein, D., Ludvigson, E., Sankar, K., Diamond, S., Morrow, M.: Blueprint for the intercloud-protocols and formats for cloud computing interoperability. In: 2009 Fourth International Conference on Internet and Web Applications and Services ICIW 2009, pp. 328–336. IEEE (2009)
10. Bromberg, Y.D., Grace, P., Réveillère, L.: Starlink: runtime interoperability between heterogeneous middleware protocols. In: 2011 31st International Conference on Distributed Computing Systems (ICDCS), pp. 446–455. IEEE (2011)
11. Bromberg, Y.-D., Grace, P., Réveillère, L., Blair, G.S.: Bridging the interoperability gap: overcoming combined application and middleware heterogeneity. In: Kon, F., Kermarrec, A.-M. (eds.) Middleware 2011. LNCS, vol. 7049, pp. 390–409. Springer, Heidelberg (2011)

12. Ng, N., Yoshida, N.: Pabble: Parameterised scribble for parallel programming. In: 2014 22nd Euromicro International Conference on Parallel, Distributed and Network-Based Processing (PDP), pp. 707–714. IEEE (2014)
13. Abramsky, S.: Computational interpretations of linear logic. Theoret. Comput. Sci. **111**(1), 3–57 (1993)

Verification and Validation of Formal Data-Centric Business Models

Timur Umarov[✉], Rustem Kamun, Askhat Omarov, and Sanzhar Altayev

Department of Management Information Systems,
Kazakh-British Technical University, 59, Tole bi str., Almaty 050000, Kazakhstan
t.umarov@kbtu.kz, {r.kamun,askhat.omarov91,altayev}@gmail.com

Abstract. This paper addresses the problem of describing and analysing internally consistent data within business process workflow specifications. We use Rodin platform for verifying the correctness of the Event-B models. These models we obtain from an ontology and an associated set of normative rules by applying mapping rules. The latter enable us to transform these specifications into Event-B modular artefacts. The resulting model, by virtue of the Event-B formalism, is very close to a typical loosely coupled component-based implementation of a business system workflow, but has the additional value of being amenable to theorem proving techniques to check and refine data representation with respect to process evolution. In this paper, we give a formal account of the design specifications defined by Event-B modules and perform verification and validation by using theorem proving techniques provided by Rodin platform.

Keywords: Event-B · Verification · Validation · Business process · Formal specifications · Rodin platform

1 Introduction

Business process management (BPM) is a challenging aspect of the enterprise. Middleware support for BPM, as provided by, for example, Oracle, Biztalk and the recent Windows Workflow Framework, has met some challenges with respect to performance and maintenance of workflow, which can be directly related to the efficiency of business modeling in terms of preserving semantics. The process of developing business models often leaves out meeting a requirement of specifying *data* in workflows, but mainly defines dataflow.

The central challenge to BPM is complexity: business processes are becoming widely distributed, interoperating across a range of inter- and intra-organizational vocabularies and semantics. It is important that complex business workflows are checked and analysed for optimality and trustworthiness prior to deployment. The problem becomes worse when we consider the enterprise's demand to regularly adapt and change processes. For example, the growth of a company, changes to the market, revaluation of tasks to minimize cost. All these

© Springer International Publishing Switzerland 2015
R. Horne (Ed.): EGC 2015, CCIS 514, pp. 134–147, 2015.
DOI: 10.1007/978-3-319-25043-4_13

factors require re-engineering or adaptation of business processes and continuous improvement of individual activities for achieving dramatic improvements of performance critical parameters such as quality (of a product or service), cost, and speed [1]. Re-engineering of a complex workflow implementation is dangerous, due to existing dependencies between tasks.

Martin Hepp, et al. [2] are emphasising the notion of *workflow-centricity* of business processes, the main weakness of which is the focus exclusively on control flow patterns. The workflow-centricity is particularly true for BPEL. This brings a major disadvantage to such workflows: it becomes impossible to access a business process space at the knowledge level which could potentially facilitate discovering of processes or their fragments for serving particular purposes. It is also impossible to query process space at the semantic level, e.g., using logical expressions and machine reasoning, which could help automate tasks execution.

Formal methods can assist in meeting the challenge of complexity, as their mathematical basis enable us to analyze and refine a system specification. Petri nets [9] are famous for modeling and analyzing business processes. However, complex systems often involve a number of different aspects that entail separate kinds of analysis and, consequently, the use of a number of different formal methods. When using formal methods engineers define specifications and attempt to prove their correctness applying a range of different tools. Verification of the specifications in this case is useful for it ensures that the system under question is internally consistent. It gives the engineers a sense of confidence that the developed specifications are error free and can operate correctly when implemented in a programming language. Validation is the process of ensuring that the developed specification is in line with the wishes of the clients. In other words, developers check the specifications against the unstructured and informal documentations of requirements.

This paper is a part of the research in which we develop an MDA transformation from normative requirements to formal designs. This type of transformation is high level and requires use of non-trivial mapping rules. In what follows, we describe an approach of using Event-B as a formal language for describing the design patterns of the system and demonstrate how these specifications can be checked for consistency. Additionally, we are outlining our future work of roundtrip engineering, by which we can detect inconsistencies in high level normative specifications.

The paper proceeds as follows:

- Section 2 provides a brief introduction to Event-B specifications and provides its formal account by focusing on the definitions of context and machines;
- Section 3 then outlines a discussion on soundness of transformation, definitions for normative requirements and gives a description on verification and validation of the generated design specifications;
- Section 4 discusses the future work towards the concept of "roundtrip engineering" for ensuring correctness of the requirements specifications.

2   Event-B

In this section, we are describing a formal language which represents a recent evolution of the B-method, and is inspired by the action systems approach [5] and oriented towards specifying and reasoning about systems that behave in a concurrent and discrete manner. This language is used to define a semantically enriched and consistent model that we obtain from our requirements specifications. We further explicate the model that is obtained by virtue of the model-driven transformation from normative requirements and regard it as a target Event-B model of the enterprise system.

2.1   Background

The process of building computer systems that behave correctly, do not involve heavy post-implementation testing and maintenance efforts, and are free of impossible executions, represents a difficult task that is normally approached by initiating software development projects with the simplest and most general specifications. These specifications are more often regarded to as artefacts or models of future systems. These models are by no means executable and therefore must not be considered as systems themselves but they help us to specify the properties and the behavior of the system to be implemented. As [6] puts it, the model of a program and more generally of a complex computer system, although non-executable, allows one to clearly identify the properties of the future system and to prove that they will be present in it.

This approach is embraced by the formal language used for modeling and reasoning about systems that behave in a discrete fashion. The notion of discrete modeling is referred to as *Event-B*. The Event-B language allows one to describe and model systems that are operated as an execution of successive concurrent states. Event-B has an operational semantics based upon predicate transformer semantics, with its origin in the Floyd-Hoare Logic of Dijkstra [7] and abstract state machines [8]. The number of possible states that the system can be in is enormous and the frequency of their occurrences is very high. Therefore, the behavior of such systems is observed as continuous, but this does not change the very nature of the problem: such systems are intrinsically discrete [6].

In general, Event-B can define a number of different contexts, that serve the same role as an algebraic theory in mathematics. For example, we might define one context to describe the structure and axioms for the theory of boolean values, and another context for the structure and axioms of the natural numbers. The definition for context is as follows.

Definition 1 (Event-B Context). *A well-formed Event-B context C for a set of variables is a tuple*

$$C = \langle \Sigma_C, \mathit{Var}, A_C \rangle$$

where

- Σ_C *is a signature.*
- $A_C = \{A_1, ..., A_m\}$ *is a set of axioms consisting of well-formed formulas of* $WFF_\Sigma(Var)$ *containing no free variables* $(FV(A_i) = \emptyset$ *for* $i = 1, ..., m)$.

We now define the form of the Event-B machines that we consider in this paper.

Definition 2 (Event-B Machine). *A well-formed Event-B machine* M *is a tuple*

$$M = \langle N_M, C_M, Var_M, I_M, E_M \rangle$$

where

- N_M *is a unique name for the machine*
- C_M *is a context for the machine* $\langle \Sigma, Var_C, A_C \rangle$
- Var_M *is a set of* state *variables* $\{a_1, ..., a_j\} = Var_M$ *disjoint from* Var_C. *Disjointedness ensures that we can use variables from the set* Var_C *as variables to be bound by existential and universal quantifiers in formulas, while variables from* Var_M *are employed exclusively to denote mutable state variables of the machine, whose values affect and are affected by the triggering of events.*
- $I_M = \{inv_1, ..., inv_k\}$ *is a set of invariants consisting of well-formed formulas of* $WFF_\Sigma(Var_M \cup Var_C)$ *so that* $FV(inv_i) \subseteq Var_M$ *and* $BV(inv_i) \cap Var_M = \varnothing$ $(i = 1, ..., k)$, *where* BV *stands for bound variables. The last two conditions ensure all variables used from* Var_C *in each invariant is quantified, but state variables are never quantified.*
- E_M *is a set of* events, *of the form*

$$\begin{array}{l} Event\ e_i \mathrel{\widehat{=}} \\ \quad WHEN\ G_i \\ \quad THEN\ S_i \\ \quad END \end{array}$$

where for some $i \geqslant 0$, *each* e_i *is a unique event name,* G_i *is a set of* guard *formulas taken from* $WFF_\Sigma(Var_M \cup Var_C)$ *and* S_M *is a* substitution *taken from* $Subst_\Sigma(Var_M)$. *As with the invariants, we require that the only free variables of each guard are state variables and that state variables are never bound: that is* $FV(G_i) \subseteq Var_M$ *and* $BV(inv_i) \cap Var_M = \varnothing$ *for* $i = 1, ..., l$.

The machine M *is written in Event-B notation as follows:*

Machine N_M
    Var $a_1, ..., a_j$ Event $e_1 \mathrel{\widehat{=}}$ ...   Event $e_l \mathrel{\widehat{=}}$
    Inv $inv_1, ..., inv_k$ WHEN G_1 WHEN G_l
                        THEN S_1 THEN S_l
                        END   END

Without loss of generality, it is assumed that all Event-B machines are defined with respect to some overall single context C and a contextual signature Σ.

3   Verification and Validation

Any Event-B specification does not guarantee correctness or consistency. We can easily write an inconsistent specification by, for example, adding an axioms of the form $0 = 0$ and $0 \neq 0$ to a context that includes the usual axioms for natural numbers. Again, it is not possible to automatically detect inconsistencies in a specification. It is up to a specification expert to ultimately ensure the specification is consistent. However, given a specification S (a set of machines) of the form $S = \{M_1, \ldots, M_n\}$, a number of properties can be set that, if proven, ensure a safer, more trustworthy specification. In particular, given a specification, it is important to prove

- Well-formedness of any functional application and relational statements. Well-formedness of function application and relational assertions is taken as a *semantic* property of the model of statements, rather than being treated syntactically as in a typed formalism. However, by examining definitions of sets and set memberships given by invariants and the context of a specification, it is possible to prove that all function applications and relational assertions are well-formed. Such a proof entails that all models of the specification will always interpret function applications and relations as appropriate.
- Invariant preservation. By proving that all invariants are entailed by both guards and substitutions of all events, it is possible to show that a specification satisfies its invariants.

Because interpretations are given over set theory, these proofs can be done using the axioms of set theory. Toolkits like Rodin will automatically generate proof obligations for these conditions from a specification and allow an interactive, tactic-based approach to proving proof obligations. One of the motivations behind mapping *requirements* specifications into Event-B *design* specifications is that toolkits like Rodin will then be of assistance in improving trustworthiness of designs by generating and discharging these types of proof obligations, prior to implementation.

3.1   Soundness of Transformation

The language proposed to define our source model is somewhat more complex, due to its relational nature and conformance to an ontology. However, we need not study the full set of formulas given: we *restrict* our attention to a subset of normative formulas that correspond to the informal schema for behavioural norms. Due to its complexity, in what follows we provide its short definition.

A Detour to MEASUR's Normative Tableaux. A MEASUR normative definition takes the following form [3]:

if *trigger* occurs and the *pre-condition is satisfied,*

then *agent* performs an action so that *post-condition*

is Obliged/Permitted/Impermissible from resulting.

Definition 3 (Formal Behavioral Norms for an Ontology). *The set of* behavioral norms *is defined to be any formula of the form*

$$G \rightarrow E_a \mathbf{D} Post \tag{1}$$

where

- $\mathbf{D}$ *is a deontic operator Ob or Pe.*
- *The only free variables occurring in G and DEF are agent or entity variables from Var_{AGENT} and Var_{ENTITY}.*

The idea of a behavioral norm is to associate knowledge and information with agents, who produce and are responsible for it. From a philosophical perspective, truth is then defined as something that an agent brings about and is responsible for. From the perspective of determining how to implement a normative ontology as a workflow-based system, we view agents as corresponding to subsystems, business entities to specifications of data and behavioral norms to expected dynamic interaction protocols between subsystems.

MEASUR [3] and, in particular, our logical restriction of MEASUR, allows much flexibility when detailing the intended meaning of communication acts. This can be done by clarifying assertions. When it comes to the question of implementation of a communication act, an analyst will always ask the client: what is entailed by this act? The client will then explain what changes the act is expected to make on the elements of the ontology.

We can encode this description as a *definition DEF* of the act A, of the form

$$A \rightarrow DEF \tag{2}$$

and

$$DEF \rightarrow A \tag{3}$$

henceforth abbreviated as

$$A \leftrightarrow DEF \tag{4}$$

where *DEF* is any MEASUR formula not involving communication acts, both A and *DEF* sharing the same free variables.

We are now ready to define our formal notion of a MEASUR requirement analysis document. Essentially, it consists of an ontology and pairs of behavioral norms and definitions, called normative tableaux.

Definition 4 (Normative Tableaux). *A requirements specification prescribes the action an agent is obliged (or permitted) to perform given the preconditions hold and consists of pairs of behavioural norms, each paired with definitions of the form*

$$REQ = \{(G_i \rightarrow E_{b\ i}\ D_i\ A_i, A_i \leftrightarrow DEF_i) \mid i = 1, \ldots, n\} \tag{5}$$

where

- G_i *represents a guard (or a pre-condition) of a given norm;*
- $E_b{}_i$ *Ob A_i is taken from the later definitions of the theory of normative positions in [12] and denotes a relativised modal sentence to stand for "agent b sees to it (or brings it about) that Ob A_i (is the case)";*
- *Ob is a deontic operator for "obligatory" and the expression Ob A_i effectively means that a single communication act A_i should obligatorily be true;*
- *DEF is any MEASUR formula not involving communication acts, both A and DEF sharing the same free variables.*

Each pair is called a normative tableaux.
    A model is a set of normative rules for a set of variables and agents. It is denoted as $\mathcal{M}$ is said to satisfy REQ if it validates the quantified conjunction of all REQ's normative tableaux. That is, $\mathcal{M}$ satisfies REQ when

$$\mathcal{M} \models \begin{pmatrix} \forall\, x_1 : T_1 \bullet \ldots, x_n : T_k \bullet \\ G_1 \rightarrow E_{b_1} \, D_1 \, A_1 \land A_1 \leftrightarrow DEF_1 \\ \land \ldots \land \\ G_n \rightarrow E_{b_n} \, D_1 \, A_n \land A_n \leftrightarrow DEF_n \end{pmatrix} \tag{6}$$

where $x_1 : T_1, \ldots, x_n : T_k$ is the list of all free variables contained in the formulas of the tableaux and the heavy dots are the dividers between the declarations and the predicates.

Preservation of Typing Theorem for Event-B. From the B research community perspective let us attempt to prove a number of desirable properties of ϕ that define how it provides an adequate semantics for MEASUR. Formal transformation of a norm is provided in [4]. The complete semantic preservation theorem and the proof that the design implementations preserve requirements are described in [10].
    Before the theorem we need to define well-formed formulas.

Definition 5 (Well-Formed Formulas). *The* basic *well-formed formulas of Event-B with signature Σ over variables Var, $BWFF_\Sigma(Var)$, take the form*

$$S_1 \subseteq S_2$$

$$S_1 \subset S_2$$

$$e \in S$$

$$e_1 = e_2$$

$$P(e_1, e_2)$$

for any $P \in C_\Sigma$. $e, e_1, e_2 \in Term_\Sigma(Var)$, $S, S_1, S_2 \in \hat{S}_\Sigma$.
    The well-formed formulas of Event-B with signature Σ over variables Var, $WFF_\Sigma(Var)$ are defined recursively:

- if $F \in BWFF_\Sigma(Var)$ then $F \in WFF_\Sigma(Var)$
- if $F_1, F_2 \in WFF_\Sigma(Var)$ then $F_1 \wedge F_2, F_1 \to F_2, \neg F_1 \in WFF_\Sigma(Var)$
- if $FWFF_\Sigma(Var)$ and $x \in Var$ then $\forall x.F, \exists x.F \in WFF_\Sigma(Var)$

Theorem 1 (Preservation of Typing). *Assume REQ is a set of behavioral norm/definition pairs over an ontology O as defined in the Definition 4 each of the form*

$$REQ = \{(G_i \to E_{b\ i}\ Ob\ A_i, A_i \leftrightarrow DEF_i) \mid i = 1, \ldots, n\} \tag{7}$$

Let S be the set of machines generated by applying a model-driven transformation function ϕ over each norm in REQ

$$S = \phi(REQ) \tag{8}$$

so that S consists of $BWFF_\Sigma(Var)$ formulas, where Var are taken from the agent and entity variables of O and Σ is taken from the signature of O.

Consider any norm/definition pair (otherwise referred to as 'tableaux' in [11]) defined as

$$N = (G \to E_{b:B\{\ldots\}}\ \mathbf{M}\ A, A \leftrightarrow DEF) \in REQ \tag{9}$$

where $\mathbf{M}$ is a modality operator taken from deontic logic. Then

- *Given any agent variable $\vdash_O a : A\{\ldots\}$ occurring in N, there is a machine M_a where M_a is the machine in S corresponding to a.*
- *Given any entity variable $\vdash_O e : E\{l_1 : T_1, \ldots, l_n : T_n\}$ occurring in REQ, we can use the notation of delimiters to denote that the following expressions are located in machine M_b:*

$$\ulcorner e \in E \urcorner \in M_b$$

$$\ulcorner f_1 \in E \to T_1 \urcorner \in M_b$$

$$\ldots$$

$$\ulcorner f_n \in E \to T_n \urcorner \in M_b$$

Proof. By inspection of each of the cases in the transformation.

Definition 6. *Assume REQ is a set of behavioral norm/definition pairs, each of the form (7). Let S be the set of machines generated by applying ϕ over each norm in REQ (8). Given a model $\mathcal{M}$ of a S, we define a state σ of $\mathcal{M}$ to be a non-intermediate state if, and only if, $\mathcal{M}, \sigma \models R_N = \bot$ for any flag variable R_N, any norm $N \in REQ$. Flag variable R_N is a shared variable of type boolean that serves as a flag between two communicating agents.*

Because inter-agent communication is always modeled using the boolean flag variables, each of the form R_N (any norm N), a non-intermediate state denotes the state of the system that is not between stages of transmission of information from one machine to another via the shared flag variables.

Assumption 1. *We will be assuming all flag variables are initialized to be $\perp$ within any initial state of the transition semantics. That is, we will assume a machine always begins in a non-intermediate stage: a reasonable assumption.*

Lemma 1. *Assume REQ is a set of behavioral norm/definition pairs, each of the form (7) Let S be the set of machines generated by applying ϕ over each norm in REQ (8). Take any model $\mathcal{M}$ that satisfies S. Consider any norm/definition tableaux of the form (9). If we have a state σ and σ' such that the model transformation of the definition provides a shift in the state from σ to σ': $\sigma' = [\phi(DEF)]\sigma$; then we know that*

$$\mathcal{M}, \sigma' \models \mathsf{toB}(DEF)$$

where $\mathsf{toB}(DEF)$ is a B representation (written in Event-B) of the definition.

Proof. By a straightforward induction over the possible forms of DEF, using the definition of ϕ.

We are now ready to show an important soundness property of the transformation. The intuitive meaning of a norm $G \to E_{b:B\{...\}}\ Ob\ A$ is that, given G holds, the agent b *must* make A hold. Because we map G to a guard and A to an action of a particular event and b to a machine that contains the event, we would expect ϕ to preserve this intuitive meaning: that is, we would expect that whenever the guard corresponding to G is satisfied, the *machine* corresponding to b *must* always perform the action associated with A.

We prove this now, formally.

Theorem 2. *Assume REQ is a set of behavioral norm/definition pairs, each of the form (7). Let S be the set of machines generated by applying ϕ over each norm in REQ (8). Take any model $\mathcal{M}$ that satisfies S. Consider any norm/definition tableaux of the form (9). For any non-intermediate state σ of $\mathcal{M}$ such that*

$$\mathcal{M}, \sigma \models \mathsf{toB}(G)$$

there is a transition to state σ' caused by event $event_N \in M_B$ such that

$$\langle S, \sigma \rangle \xrightarrow{*} \langle S, \sigma_1 \rangle \xrightarrow{*} \ldots \xrightarrow{*} \langle S, \sigma_n \rangle \xrightarrow{M_B, event_N} \langle S, \sigma' \rangle$$

where we know that the B machine interpretation of A's definition becomes true in state σ'

$$\mathcal{M}, \sigma' \models \mathsf{toB}(DEF)$$

Proof. We use the definition of ϕ and the transitional semantics of B machines. There are two cases, depending on the form of A.

- If A is of the form $R(p, b', b)$, where $p : P\{...\}$, $P\{...\} \in ENTITY$, $b : B\{...\}$, $B\{...\} \in AGENT$, $b' : B'\{...\}$, $B'\{...\} \in AGENT$ and $R \in COMMACT$ (type for communication acts used in the requirements definitions) and where the two agent types are *different*, so $B\{\ldots\} \neq B'\{\ldots\}$, then we take the post-condition $E_b\ Ob\ R(p, b', b)$, in which case by the definition of ϕ we know that there is an event named $event_N$ in the machine $M_B \in S$ of the form

$$
\ulcorner Event\ event_N \mathrel{\widehat{=}} \qquad\qquad \urcorner \\
\quad \text{WHEN } GUARD_N(G)^* \qquad \in E_{M_B} \\
\quad \text{THEN } \phi_N(DEF);\ R_N := \perp \\
\quad \text{END}
\tag{10}
$$

where

$$
GUARD_N(G)^* \equiv GUARD_N(G)/G' \wedge R_N = \top \equiv
$$
$$
(\mathsf{toB}(G)/G') \wedge R_N = \top \tag{11}
$$

and there is an event $comEvent_N$ in machine $M_{B'}$:

$$
\ulcorner Event\ comEvent_N \mathrel{\widehat{=}} \urcorner \\
\quad \text{WHEN } G'_N \qquad \in E_{M_{B'}}, \\
\quad \text{THEN } R_N := \top \\
\quad \text{END}
\tag{12}
$$

where $G' \equiv GUARD_N(G)\,|_{ExtVAR(M_{B'})} \equiv \mathsf{toB}(G)\,|_{ExtVAR(M_{B'})}$. Now, assuming a state σ such that

$$
\mathcal{M}, \sigma \models \mathsf{toB}(G) \tag{13}
$$

it *cannot* be the case that $\mathcal{M}, \sigma \models GUARD_N(G)^*$ holds by (11), because

$$
\mathcal{M}, \sigma \models R_N = \perp
$$

by assumption. However, by (13) it must be the case that $\mathcal{M}, \sigma \models G'_N$ (because $G'_N \equiv GUARD_N(G)\,|_{ExtVAR(M_{B'})}$, and the restricted form of a conjunctive formula should hold if the original formula holds over a state). Consequently, we know that

$$
\langle S, \sigma \rangle \overset{M_{B'}, comEvent_N}{\longrightarrow} \langle S, \sigma_1 \rangle
$$

where $\sigma_1 = [R_{call} := \top]\sigma$. So

$$
\mathcal{M}, \sigma_1 \models R_{call} = \top \tag{14}
$$

Furthermore, because all other events are generated from norms that exclude each other's guards, σ_1 is the *only* such state that can follow from σ. By (13) and the fact that G (and so toB) do not contain any reference to R_N, we have

$$
\mathcal{M}, \sigma_1 \models \mathsf{toB}(G) \tag{15}
$$

But then it must be the case that

$$
\mathcal{M}, \sigma_1 \models GUARD_N(G)^* \tag{16}
$$

by (11), (14) and (15) because $GUARD_N(G)^* \equiv (\text{toB}(G)/G') \wedge R_N = \top$. Finally, by definition of the executable semantics, we know that there is a state σ' such that

$$\langle S, \sigma_1 \rangle \overset{M_B, event_N}{\to} \langle S, \sigma' \rangle$$

where $\sigma' = [\phi(D); R_{call} := \bot]\sigma_1$ and so, by Lemma 1, $\mathcal{M}, \sigma' \models \text{toB}(DEF)$. Furthermore, because all other events are generated from norms that exclude each other's guards, σ' is the *only* such state that can follow from σ_1, as required.

– The proof is very similar for the case where $R(p, b', b)$, where $p : P\{\ldots\}$, $P\{\ldots\} \in ENTITY$, $b : B\{\ldots\}$, $B\{\ldots\} \in AGENT$, $b' : B'\{\ldots\}$, $B'\{\ldots\} \in AGENT$ and $R \in COMMACT$ and where the two agent types are *the same*, so $B\{\ldots\} = B'\{\ldots\}$. The main difference is that the transitions are occurring within the same machine, rather than out of it – however this does not effect the argument over the transition semantics, which is essentially the same as the dual machine case above. The main difference is that the transitions are occurring within the same machine, rather than out of it – however this does not effect the argument over the transition semantics, which is essentially the same as the dual machine case above.

The analogous case for the *Pe* modality holds similarly.

3.2   Validation of the Specification

One of the requirements of formal specifications is to prove that they are internally consistent. We are particularly interested in checking whether assignment statements of events preserve the guards and invariants of the generated Event-B model. The Event-B language (similarly to B-method) defines proof obligations for substitutions (or events). Discharging these proof obligations presents a form of specification validation.

For the purposes of validation of our specifications we have used the Rodin platform. The Rodin platform is an extensible application for refinements and mathematical proofs in Event-B, which is based on the Eclipse integrated development environment. Figures 1 and 2 show our Event-B specifications in the Rodin platform.

Let us now illustrate the *proving* perspective of the Rodin platform. Table 1 shows that 12 proof obligations were proven automatically. Formal designs with proof obligations that are proven automatically are said to be well-specified. For example, proof obligation of event *receive_order* is the following predicate:

$$
\begin{aligned}
&(1) \quad status \in Order \to STATUS \wedge \\
&(2) \quad receive\_order_{call} = \top \wedge \neg oo \in ordered \\
&\qquad\quad \Rightarrow \\
&(3) \quad status \lhd \{oo \mapsto received\} \in Order \to STATUS
\end{aligned}
\tag{17}
$$

```
MACHINE                          INVARIANTS
    E                            inv1   :   receive_order_call ∈ BOOL
SEES                             inv2   :   oo ∈ Order
    EOS_C                        inv3   :   ordered ⊆ Order
                                 inv4   :   status ∈ Order → STATUS
VARIABLES                        inv5   :   processing ∈ BOOL
    receive_order_call           inv6   :   ordered_by ⊆ Order
    oo                           inv7   :   total ∈ Order→N
    ordered                      inv8   :   limit ∈ N
    status                       inv9   :   process_successful_call ∈ BOOL
    processing                   inv10  :   process_unsuccessful_call ∈ BOOL
    ordered_by                   inv11  :   invoice_if_available_call ∈ BOOL
    total                        inv12  :   in_stock ∈ BOOL
    limit                        inv13  :   order_invoiced ∈ BOOL
    process_successful_call      inv14  :   dispatch_order_call ∈ BOOL
    process_unsuccessful_call    inv15  :   reject_order_call ∈ BOOL
    invoice_if_available_call    inv16  :   request_increase_call ∈ BOOL
    in_stock
    order_invoiced
    dispatch_order_call
    reject_order_call
    request_increase_call
```

Fig. 1. Variables and invariants of machine *e* represented in the Rodin platform

```
EVENTS

receive_order    ≙                   process_successful    ≙
WHICH IS                             WHICH IS
    ordinary                             ordinary
WHEN                                 WHEN
    grd1  :  receive_order_call=TRUE     grd1  :  process_successful_call=TRUE
    grd2  :  oo∉ordered                  grd2  :  oo∈ordered
THEN                                     grd3  :  processing=TRUE
    act1  :  ordered=ordered∪{oo}        grd4  :  total(oo)<limit
    act2  :  ordered_by=ordered_by∪{oo}  grd5  :  status(oo)=received
    act3  :  status(oo)=received     THEN
    act4  :  processing=TRUE             act1  :  status(oo)=pending
    act5  :  receive_order_call=FALSE    act2  :  process_successful_call=FALSE
END                                  END
```

Fig. 2. Events *receive_order* and *process_successful* of machine *e* represented in the Rodin platform

This predicate means that given invariant (1) and guards (2) hold, the assignment expression $status(oo) := received$ applied to the invariant must also hold (3). According to Table 1, all 12 generated proof obligations for machine *e* were proven automatically. It is important to define specifications which provide proof obligations that are easy for the theorem provers to discharge. Otherwise the specifications have to be rewritten in a different manner which helps simplify the proving process.

Table 1. Proof obligations

Machine	Proof obligations	Automatic	Interactive
e	12	12	0

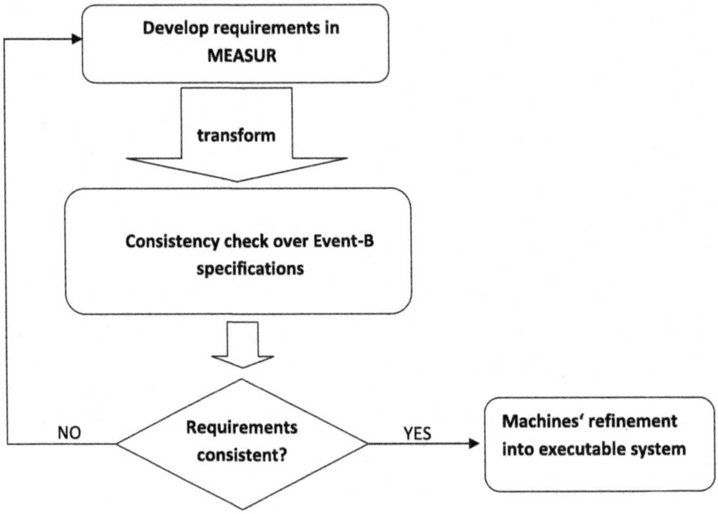

Fig. 3. Roundtrip engineering concept for our transformation

4 Conclusion

The contributions described in this paper are substantial and cutting-edge, thereby advancing the state-of-the-art of BPM. We have defined a consistent B machine and operational semantics for Event-B (referred as a platform independent model in our approach). The operational semantics was formally defined by an Event-B specification, models and interpretations and the state of a machine. We have also defined a notion of state transition by virtue of describing generalised substitution and transitional semantics, and we have provided a definition of invariant preservation and model satisfaction. Our approach is one of the few attempts to formally embed semantics to the requirements specification via MDA and provide an operational semantics of Event-B to the behavioral part of the normative specifications.

By virtue of implementing a transformation and generating an Event-B modules we have provided a formal semantics for the normative ontologies (see [10,11] for details on normative ontologies) with correctness and validity in mind. The generated Event-B specification are further checked for consistency and the respective proof obligations are discharged. These modular specifications can further be used in refining to more detailed implementations.

As a future work we argue that our method can potentially be used to automatically detect faults and inconsistencies in the normative requirements. The concept is illustrated in Fig. 3. According to this diagram, if the requirements are consistent, then the generated Event-B models from these requirements can be used for further refinement stages in order to obtain an executable system. In the cases of faults in the requirements, we plan to implement "roundtrip engineering". If there are inconsistencies in the specifications, the generated Event-B design models will have these inconsistencies embedded, which can be detected by the Rodin platform. The requirements should be revisited and checked in order to eliminate these faults. This is a subject of our future scientific inquiry.

References

1. van der Aalst, W., van Hee, K.: Workflow Management: Models, Methods, and Systems. The MIT Press, Cambridge (2002)
2. Hepp, M., Roman, D.: An ontology framework for semantic business process management. In: Proceedings of the 8th International Conference Wirtschaftsinformatik Universitaetsverlag Karlsruhe (2007)
3. Liu, K.: Semiotics in Information Systems Engineering. Cambridge University Press, Cambridge (2000)
4. Poernomo, I., Umarov, T.: A mapping from normative requirements to event-b to facilitate verified data-centric business process management. In: Szmuc, T., Szpyrka, M., Zendulka, J. (eds.) CEE-SET 2009. LNCS, vol. 7054, pp. 136–149. Springer, Heidelberg (2012)
5. Back, R.-J.: Refinement calculus, part II: parallel and reactive programs. In: de Bakker, J.W., de Roever, W.-P., Rozenberg, G. (eds.) Stepwise Refinement of Distributed Systems. LNCS, vol. 430, pp. 67–93. Springer, Heidelberg (1990)
6. Abrial, J.-R., Métayer, C., Voisin, L.: Event-B language. RODIN Deliverable 3.2 (2005)
7. Dijkstra, E.: Guarded commands, nondeterminacy and formal derivation of program. Commun. ACM **18**(8), 453–457 (1975)
8. Gurevich, Y., Kutter, P., Odersky, M., Thiele, L. (eds.): ASM 2000. LNCS, vol. 1912. Springer, Heidelberg (2000)
9. Wolfgang, R.: Petri Nets: An Introduction. Springer, Heidelberg (1985)
10. Poernomo, I., Umarov, T.: Implementing a sound mapping from normative requirements to event-b design blueprints using MDA. In: Proceedings of the 2012 International Conference on Software Engineering Research & Practice. CSREA Press (2012)
11. Kamun, R., Omarov, A., Umarov, T.: Business Requirements: Normative Approach to Behavior Modeling Proceedings of the 4th International Symposium on Business Modeling and Software Design (2014)
12. Jones, A., Sergot, M.: On the characterization of law and computer systems: the normative systems perspective. In: Meyer, J.-J.C., Wieringa, R.J. (eds.) Deontic Logic in Computer Science: Normative System Specification, pp. 275–307. Wiley, Chichester (1993)

Author Index

Printed in the United States
By Bookmasters